SOLOMON

The King with a Listening Heart

Studies in 1 Kings 1-13

Walter C. Kaiser, Jr.

Lederer Books
An imprint of
Messianic Jewish Publishers
Clarksville, MD 21029

Printed in the United States of America

Cover design by Lisa Rubin,
Messianic Jewish Publishers
Graphic Design by Yvonne Vermillion,
Magic Graphix, Westfork, Arkansas

2025 1

ISBN: 978-1-951833-06-0

Published by:
Lederer Books
An imprint of Messianic Jewish Publishers
6120 Day Long Lane
Clarksville, MD 21029

Distributed by:
Messianic Jewish Publishers & Resources
Order line: (800) 410-7367
lederer@messianicjewish.net
www.MessianicJewish.net

To my beloved wife Nancy Elizabeth
for her love and care of me and
her four wonderful children:
Lisa
Tamala
Steven
Scott

Table of Contents

Lesson 1

The Coronation of Solomon

1 Kings 1:1-2:12

The first two chapters of 1 Kings are truly transitional, for they mark the move from the rule of King David to the next in line in his family, King Solomon. Critical scholars love to see these two chapters, not as the beginning of 1 Kings, but as the "conclusion" to the so-called "Succession Narrative" that stretches from 2 Samuel 9-20 to 1 Kings 1-2. But this is a scholarly invention rather than a Scriptural designation. But our focus is more on the character and life of Solomon as presented in these Scriptures.

The time is about 970 B.C.E. and the first four verses of 1 Kings 1:1-4 seem to paint a picture of a King David who "was old and well advanced in years" (1:1) and having trouble "keep[ing] warm even when they put covers over him" (1:1). King David appears to have little zest for life in his senior years, with a result that matters of state were beginning to slip and events were about to preempt any wish or instruction David might give about who was to be the future king. It was time someone acted and that person seems to have been Nathan the prophet (1:11).

This narrative in 1 Kings 1:1 – 2:12, that takes us from a possible insurrection of power in the Davidic monarchy to the death of King David, can be covered in five major scenes: (1) David's son Adonijah puts himself forward as the new leader asserting, "I will be king," (1:1-10); (2) the prophet Nathan and David's Queen Bathsheba halt Adonijah's quest for the throne by pleading with King David to act immediately and decisively on naming a successor (1:11-27); (3) David, therefore, declares Solomon to be king (28-40); (4) Adonijah's coronation festivities are suddenly halted with the news of Solomon's installation as king in Israel (1:41-53); and (5) King David's charge to Solomon and David's death (2:1-12). So let us go directly to the text to examine the character and life of Solomon.

There are four provisions that God gave to David and to us that provided a successor to rule on the throne of Israel.

    I.   The Provision of an Incentive to Act – 1:1-1

    II. The Provision of an Alternative Plan – 1:11-27

    III. The Provision to Install Solomon as King – 1:28-40

    IV. The Provision of Making the Kingdom Secure – 2:1-12

The Provision of an Incentive to Act – 1:1-10

As the death of David was about to take place, things were beginning to get a little out of hand in Israel due to David's laxity in administering the affairs of the government. Two of David's sons seem to have been in line to be the next king, Adonijah and Solomon, but David was showing real signs of slowing down and being somewhat out of what was going on around him. In fact, he was not even being "cool about it;" instead, he was just plain "cold" in every way, for he was having trouble even getting body warmth, much less his thinking. As a result, his servants decided to look for a "young virgin" who could attend to the king and "lie beside him so that … [he might] keep warm" (2b). The text makes clear that this was strictly a method of supplying David with a form of heat therapy (sort of like his hot water bottle or blanket) and had nothing to do with any sexual prowess on David's part (4b). The woman the servants selected to supply this needed heat to the aging monarch David was the beautiful Abishag, a young woman from the town of Shunem.

While David was all wrapped up in himself, and his need to get some warmth, a precarious moment was building outside in the nation, without any input or leadership from David as king. David's son Adonijah had presumptuously put himself forward with his own declaration: "I will be king" (5).

Now it is important to notice that the Biblical writer said that "His father had never interfered with him by asking, 'Why do you behave as you do?'" (6). To add to this deficit, "[Adonijah] also was handsome and was born next in line after Absalom" (6b). Thus, in these brief vignettes, we are given clues that Adonijah was so terribly ambitious (5a), that he also showed some pompous *style* in the way he got designated horses and chariots along with 50 men to run ahead of him to clear his line of travel (5b), along with the image and position he sported (6b, 6c), not to mention the political and military support that he had raised up to back him candidacy for kingship (7, 9). All this spelled danger and a real threat for the Davidic throne.

Adonijah's lack of parental discipline, his obvious good looks, and his increasingly large following in the path that his brother Absalom had taken in an earlier attempted coup showed he was not the best candidate to ascend the Davidic throne.

This was a moment that was filled with as much danger as any Israel had faced in the past. In fact, times of transition from one ruler to the next are almost always times of great peril, but even more so if the aspiring person has more external attractive features to offer than those of the inner heart, mind and wisdom. Adonijah's lust for power and position are not the usual marks for distinguished leadership among the people of God. Instead, they are markers of future trouble!

Adonijah had cleverly gathered to his side Joab, as his pick to lead his army and Abiathar as his choice for priest in Israel, but he had purposely left out of his entourage Zadok the priest, who was the top priest for King David. He had also decided not to choose Benaiah, one of the military bureaucrats, nor Nathan, the royal court's prophet, or even Shimei and his friends, along with David's special security guard of the Kerethites and Pelethites (7-8, 44). This list indicates that Adonijah understood that there was a marked division of power and influence within the government of David and he was ready to move quickly in a surprised coup to tilt the forces in his favor, but he must do it quickly.

But in the providence of God, these moves would be the very sorts of events, when they were rehearsed to David just in time, moves that would be used by God, to move David to take immediate steps to put an alternative plan into action.

At the Spring of En-rogel, several hundred yards south of the City of David, Adonijah had set his installation party now into full swing (9). Almost all the king's sons, his brothers, had been invited, along with all the "men of Judah, who were royal officials," to a feast in Adonijah's honor as the next king (9b). Once again, it must be stressed that Nathan the prophet had not been invited, nor had Adonijah's brother Solomon, or the military man Benaiah, or the special security guard of David, been invited either (10). The die was cast for a major coup in which some were going to lose their lives if this coup succeeded. This exclusion of these otherwise respected men showed that Adonijah was not prepared for a peaceful existence, which otherwise would have meant sudden death for all potential heirs, for in that case they would have been invited to a joint meal, but the losers would eventually need to be totally liquidated and annihilated by the opposition in order for the coup to work.

The Provision of an Alternative Plan – 1:11-27

The uninformed and aged king must now be briefed immediately on what was happening in the undercover coup, so Nathan the prophet went into action. He began by briefing Bathsheba about his plans to stop this whole affair, for as he exclaimed it to Bathsheba, he asked: "Have you not heard that Adonijah, the son of Haggith, has become king without our Lord David's knowing it?" (11). This section of the text, then, falls into three parts: (1) Nathan to Bathsheba (11-14), (2) Bathsheba to David (15-21), and (3) Nathan to David (22-27).

Nathan to Bathsheba – 1:11-14

The presumption is that David had promised on an oath that Bathsheba's son Solomon would be the next king to succeed him (17). But while David shivered in his lack of warmth and unbelievably hesitated, Adonijah saw his opportunity to move in aggressively and present Israel with a *fait accompli*. Since Solomon had not been invited to Adonijah's incarnation, Adonijah must have known that Solomon had been the favorite to succeed his father, so he had to beat his father to the punch!

It is true, of course, that Adonijah was the oldest living heir of King David, who apparently had a sudden growing popular support from the people for his candidacy, but as long as David hesitated and doodled on his sick bed, the door was opened for those who were more aggressive and speedy to preempt what he might do – and that was Adonijah's exact purpose.

Bathsheba, then according to Nathan's plan, was to go into to David's bedroom and remind him of the oath he had made to her, that her son

Solomon would be the next in line to rule after him. But if that were so, she would ask rhetorically, then why was Adonijah declaring he now was the king? (13). As if by accident, it was planned, while Bathsheba was suddenly dropping this bombshell on David about the latest news of the day, Nathan would immediately enter the bedroom of David and confirm what Bathsheba had just said (14).

Bathsheba to David – 1:15-21

Therefore, Bathsheba acted at once on Nathan's plan. She entered the bedroom of King David, where Abishag was warmly attending to the needs of an infirm David (15). Bathsheba bowed low before the king and he asked her idiomatically (in the literal Hebrew), "What to you?" as if he were barely alive and could utter but a few syllables. However, when David suddenly fully realized all that was going on, he really came alive in verse 28.

Bathsheba helped the king recall that he had promised her — that her son Solomon would be the next king. But this did not seem like it was going to happen, she teasingly implied, for now that the events that were taking place at that very moment down at the Spring of En-Rogel presented a wholly different scenario. To help King David to get moving into action, Bathsheba added that Adonijah had sacrificed man cattle, fattened calves, and sheep to help David come to grips with what really was happening right at that moment. Moreover, Adonijah had invited all the king's sons, Abiathar the priest, Joab the commander of the army. But he had not invited her son Solomon. She also added that if the king did not do something quickly, then as soon as the people of Israel had laid to rest David following his death, it was certain that both she and her son Solomon would be treated as criminals, or even worse (21). That was part of the emotional argument to help motivate David to action!

Nathan to David – 1:22-27

As planned, while Bathsheba was saying all of this to David, Nathan the prophet arrived, as if by accident. He innocently pretended to pose a question that he had no answer to: "Have you, my lord the king, declared Adonijah shall be king after you, and that he will sit on your throne?

Today he has gone down and sacrificed great numbers of cattle, fattened calves, and sheep. He has invited all the king's sons, the commanders of the army, and Abiathar the priest. In fact, right now they are eating and drinking with him and saying, 'Long live King Adonijah!'" (24-25).

Nathan carefully added that he, Zadok the priest, and Benaiah son of Jehoiada, and David's son Solomon had not been invited to the installation of this new king. It was clear that nothing but trouble lay ahead for those who had not been invited. However, Nathan continued to play dumb as he tepidly asked, "Is this something my lord the king has done without letting his servants know who should sit on the throne of my lord the king after him?" (27). Of course, Nathan knew better, but Nathan put it that way so he would arouse whatever embers of fire that were left in old David's brain to act.

The Provision to Install Solomon as King – 1:28-53

David Responds to Nathan's Plan – 1:28-40

Nathan's plan for getting David to act worked to perfection, for David was fully aroused and immediately swung into action, just as if he were the David of the former days. He immediately ordered Bathsheba to return to his court room as he then reaffirmed to Bathsheba and Nathan his previous oath to his wife about Solomon being king (28-30). Not only did he reaffirm his promise to Bathsheba about Solomon being king, but David began giving a blizzard of orders that detailed how Solomon should be immediately anointed and installed as king of Israel. Zadok the priest, Nathan the prophet, and Benaiah were to take his son Solomon at once, mounted on the king's own mule, and go down to the Gihon Spring. After they had anointed Solomon, they were to blow the trumpet and shout, "Long live King Solomon!" (33). Then these appointed officials were to bring Solomon up from Gihon and have him sit on the throne David had occupied, and he was to rule in place of David (35).

God had promised David that his dynasty would be established in perpetuity (2 Sam. 7:12-16), and that God would make David's son his own son as he, the Living God, would be a personal "Father" to him, and he would be given "a throne, a dynasty and a kingdom" that would last "forever" (2 Sam. 7:16). When David originally heard this for the first time years ago, he was so stunned and overawed that he declared, "This is the charter/instruction for all humanity." (2 Sam. 7:19; my translation). God was now promising David a continuation of the promises he had given to Eve, to Shem, to Abraham, to Isaac, and to Jacob.

But by now, David was so aroused and stirred by what was to come of his throne, kingdom, and dynasty (which institutions were not his, but the property of the coming Son of God, the Messiah), that he went into high gear. Despite the clear statement in the Davidic Covenant that all God's provisions for the future were embraced in the provisions and providence of God, yet the story that was about to unfold before them seemed merely to stress the human side of the story – or so it seemed. Adonijah's quest for the throne was fortunately met by Nathan's detailed counter plan! However, none of these matters were a surprise, or outside the providential provisions that a Lord, who is sovereign over everything, for nothing takes place on planet earth without God's knowing it and bringing it to pass. Even though the hand of God may have seemed to be invisible in this matter, since he did not intervene in any spectacular or miraculous way, such as striking down Adonijah with lightning, or giving him a sudden attack of indigestion and an unexpected death from all his partying, yet our Lord still moved the hands of men to see his will done.

Adonijah Responds to Solomon's Installation – 1:41-53

When the noise of all the celebration for Solomon's installation that was going on at the Gihon Spring as the sound of the trumpet reached Adonijah and his guests to the south of the Gihon Spring, who were just about finished with their feast (41), Joab the commander of the army asked, "What's the meaning of all the noise in the city?" With that, Jonathan, son of Abiathar the priest, arrived with some breaking news for Adonijah's guests. Adonijah invited Jonathan into the feast, hoping he carried good news as he usually always had in the past.

Jonathan announced that such a hope was not the case ("Not at all!"), for "Our lord King David has made Solomon king" (43). Jonathan must have been at the Gihon Spring to witness all these happenings, for he sure had a lot of details down cold. Zadok the priest and Nathan the prophet have anointed Solomon as king of Israel at the Gihon Spring, and they have put him on the king's mule (44). What's more, "Solomon has taken his seat on the royal throne" (47), and the royal officials are currently congratulating him saying, "May your God make Solomon's name more famous than yours (David) and his throne greater than yours!" (47). Even King David bowed in worship on his bed as he declared, "Praise be to the LORD, the God of Israel, who has allowed my eyes to see a successor on my throne today" (48).

With this alarming report, Adonijah's guests wisely decided that they should hurry home and appear to be as busy as they could be at their own work around home. While his guests fled, Adonijah, however, was just too visible. He must make a public, humiliating show of subservience to Solomon, the winner of the crown (53). For Adonijah had by now, out of fear of Solomon, taken hold of the horns of the altar, the place of sanctuary (51). Solomon's promise was that if Adonijah showed himself "to be a worthy man" (52), he would not lose one hair on his head. So, Solomon sent men to bring Adonijah from his place of sanctuary at the horns of the altar in the house of God.

The Provision of Making the Kingdom Secure – 2:1-11

To see that the throne, dynasty, and kingdom that God had given to David were made secure, some vigilant measures had to be taken. This theme of "making firm" or "secure" (Hebrew, *kun)* the throne is the theme of this second chapter (2:12, 24, 45, 46). Therefore, just as chapter one focused on the succession and transition of the kingdom, so chapter two focused on the security of the kingdom. Therefore, David, in a most dramatic death-bed scene, gave instructions to his son Solomon about ensuring the security of his kingdom (2:1-12).

Even though David was obviously quite frail at this time, he had forgotten little and therefore he reminded his son of the possible roadblocks that could occur to take away the security of his kingdom. But first Solomon was reminded that he was to "be strong and to show [him]self a man" (2:2). Furthermore, he was to "Walk in [God's] ways, and keep his decrees and commands, his laws and his requirements, as written in the Law of Moses, so that [he might] prosper in all [he] did and wherever [he] went" (3). Similar injunctions had been given to other worthy saints at the close of their lives, including: Joseph (Gen. 50:24-25), Moses (Deut. 31:1-8), and Joshua (Josh. 24:1-28). Notice all the terms used to describe all the Lord's word are very similar to the ones that he had given to Moses. If Solomon wanted to prosper, he would need to have a lifestyle (Hebrew *halak*, "walk") that was pleasing to God and one that enjoyed and obeyed the law of God if he wished to see his kingdom remain secure (2:4).

Today, few leaders of the world's nations think very much, if anything, about walking with the Lord, or being faithful in obeying his word, but that is also why there is so little security for the state of governments around the world. Therefore, let it be noted for all to follow: true stability in life can only come through obedience to the commands of the Lord, and a faithful walk with him day after day. Likewise, what is true on a personal level is also true of nations and governments: stability and longevity of a state or nation are not dependent on our experiences, professional qualifications, education, pedigree, or personal achievements alone, but fundamentally depends on our walk with God and our obedience to his word (2:4).

After David had told Solomon the most important matters for his success (2:1-4), he then gave him some advice about keeping his eye on Joab, the commander of David's army (2:5-6). Joab had killed both Abner and Amasa during peacetime and brought reproach on David's kingdom during those former days. Solomon was to deal with Joab in his wisdom, but he was not to let his grey head go down to the grave in peace, for Joab had also joined the Adonijah group.

Over against that advice, David urged Solomon to give special care and kindness to the sons of Barzillai of Gilead, for he stood by David and offered food to David's retinue when he had to flee during the insurrection of his other son Absalom (2:7; 2 Sam. 17:27-29; 19:31-40). However, David's advice on the Benjamite Shimei son of Gera was not as pleasant, for he was the one who cursed David and threw stones at him and his party as they were fleeing from Jerusalem after Absalom's sudden seizure of the throne (2:8-9; 2 Sam. 16:5-14). Solomon's rule was to be careful of his enemies and not let them repeat what they had done in the past.

David did pass away after he had reigned for forty years over Israel in the city of David – seven of those years in Hebron and thirty-three in Jerusalem (2:10-11). Thus, the reign of Solomon began.

Conclusions

1. God's provision and providence are just as apparent through the movements and actions of godly men and women as they are in his direct and miraculous interventions.

2. It is important for parents not to give free rein to their children, lest they grow up to be aspiring tyrants like Adonijah.

3. The call to leadership does not come from the east or the west, but from the Lord himself (e.g., Ps 75:6-7)

4. God is present even in the crises of life. Nothing is too big or too small for his particular attention and resolution.

5. God's command to all who would walk with him and obey his word is to "Be strong and show yourself a man."

Questions for Thought and Reflection

1. Why do you think King David faced coups from his own children on two separate occasions? Was he not as good a father as he was an administrator?

2. Was King David aware of the mischief his son Adonijah had in mind when he started to get his horses and chariot together with 50 citizens running ahead of his chariot? What role should he have taken?

3. Was David aware that Adonijah was holding an impromptu court session outside the palace to give decisions prior to the people contacting the king to curry the favor of the populace? Should he have said anything to his son?

4. What role did Nathan the prophet play in making sure that Solomon became to next king and not Adonijah?

5. Can you discern the role of divine providence in this whole administration change over from David to Solomon?

Lesson 2

Establishing Solomon's Kingdom

1 Kings 2:12-46

There can be little doubt that the theme of this chapter in 1 Kings 2 is the issue of making the kingdom given to Solomon secure. The Hebrew verb *kun*, "to make firm, be established" is used four times in this chapter (1 Kgs. 2:12, 24, 45, 46). This then provides the theme for the chapter. If the first chapter of 1 Kings focused on the succession of the kingdom in Solomon's hands, then chapter 2 of 1 Kings is concerned for the security of the kingdom.

But there is another theme in this chapter that aids in the accomplishment of maintaining that security: eight times the word death appears (1 Kgs. 2:24, 25, 26, 30, 34, 37, 42, 46). It is these deaths that help assure Solomon the establishment of his kingdom.

There is an overlap of significant answers to the question: How is Solomon's kingdom to be made secure and established? Let this chapter, then, help us to answer that question.

There are three CHANGES that need to be made if Solomon's kingdom is to be secure.

    I. Adonijah Must be Removed After He Makes a Second Play for the Kingdom

    II. Solomon Removes Abiathar the Priest and Joab Commander of Israel's Army

    III. Solomon Elevates Benaiah as Commander and Zadok as Priest

Adonijah Must be Removed After He Makes a Second Play for the Kingdom – 2:13-25

As already noted in the previous chapter, King David had instructed his son Solomon that he was to show strength and real manhood by walking in the ways of the Lord if he wanted his kingdom to be secure and established during his reign. It is true that v. 12 already had noted that "Solomon sat on the throne of his father David" and his rule was firmly established, yet the actual fact of its establishment did not come until after the threats posed against his kingdom in the rest of 1 Kings 2 had been carried out and the final word was given in v. 46c, "The kingdom was now firmly established in Solomon's hands." However, it is not that the writer of 1 Kings was confused or mixed up in his chronology of events, but this is typical of Hebrew narrative where the writer will often place this note as an anticipation of what is to come as well as a note of closure to what had preceded this event.

In the section that begins in v. 13, we note that Adonijah still does not get it: he is not the king, nor will he ever be chosen to be the king. Nevertheless, he wanted to give it one more big attempt on his part. He chose Solomon's mother Bathsheba as the best place to strike, deciding perhaps this was the weakest point in the emerging kingdom. So Adonijah paid a visit to her. She must have suspected something was up, for why would the man who had lost the kingship to her son pay a visit to her, so she asked: "Do you come peacefully?" The obvious answer to Bathsheba's question was that Adonijah had not lost his ambition and hopes for being king of Israel yet, for he was going to give those hopes one more good try.

Adonijah's interests in requesting Bathsheba to request permission to marry Abishag the Shunammite were not romantic in the least; they were first and foremost political. He wanted Solomon's mother to ask her son for his permission for him to marry the woman who had served as the woman who cuddled up close to aged King David, who was not getting warm enough from all other sources, to lie close to him to make up for that deficiency. Now one must not think immediately that Bathsheba was a somewhat naïve person who walked into this trap blindly and without any suspicions about Adonijah's motives. To the contrary, she may have been very suave about what Adonijah was up to, for she may just have decided to play along with him, knowing he, by making this request, would seal his doom. In fact, in those early days of the monarchy it was a rather ordinary thing to pass on the king's harem to his successor. Thus, even the prophet Nathan noted that Yahweh himself had given to King David, as the new king of the nation, the wives of King Saul (2 Sam. 12:8).

Likewise, Adonijah's brother, Absalom, when he attempted to overthrow his father David as king, publicly bedded the concubines that David had left in Jerusalem to show that he had now assumed the rights and status of the king of the nation (I Sam. 16:21-22). One more example may help, for Ishbosheth, one of King Saul's sons, grew extremely angry with his new general Abner, for he had taken one of Saul's concubines (2 Sam. 3:7-8), thereby raising a public signal that he thereby disputed with Ishbosheth the power of the throne with him.

It is true, of course, that the Scripture directly stated that David had no marital relations with Abishag, but her relationship to him was merely a therapeutic one whereby he got warmth from her body. Nevertheless, given her close relationship to David, she could be seen as one of David's wives.

Adonijah sort of let the cat out of the bag when he tried to add an additional reason why Bathsheba should intervene with Solomon on her behalf by saying: "As you know, the kingdom was mine. All Israel looked to me as their king. But things changed, and the kingdom has gone to my brother; for it has come to him from the LORD" (1 Kgs. 2:15).

When Bathsheba went before her son Solomon to make Adonijah's request (19-21), Solomon blew his stack! He quickly fired back, "Why do you request Abishag the Shunammite for Adonijah? You might as well request the kingdom for him – after all, he is my older brother" (22). Solomon was wise enough to see right through Adonijah's whole scheme. That man was determined to grasp the kingship one way or another.

The Scriptures do not tell us what the state of Bathsheba's mind was, for we are left without any further information. However, if she was mother to a wise son, she may also have wisely, and with a skill that some mothers have, alerted her son to the fact that his brother had not given up his idea of being king instead of Solomon.

In situations such as these, one does not wait around to see how things will play themselves out. No, instead they called Solomon to act swiftly, or he and his mother would soon be gone! Solomon immediately vowed, "May God deal with me, be it ever so severely, if Adonijah does not pay with his life for this request" (23). "Adonijah shall be put to death today" (24).

With that, Solomon ordered his new general who had replaced Joab to strike down Adonijah. That is how Adonijah came to his end (25). Of course, to some this may seem as an altogether unnecessary and harsh response, but if Solomon were to have left Adonijah loose in his realm, he would never have been able to watch him as closely as he needed to be with those kinds of aspirations on his brother's heart and mind. Solomon would have needed to tend more to this nuisance than he could have to his administrative duties or to the building projects he would carry out in the next 20 years.

Solomon Removes Abiathar the Priest and Joab the Commander of the Army – 2:26-34

There was more house-cleaning that needed to be accomplished. Solomon ordered that Abiathar be banished to his home in the priestly town of Anathoth (26). Anathoth was a mere two or three miles north of Jerusalem, the same city that the prophet Jeremiah came from later. But what Abiathar had done in supporting the coup of Adonijah made him a candidate for the sword; however, Solomon took pity on him because he had served his father David faithfully, shared in his father's hardships, and he had also carried the Ark of the Covenant in his role as High Priest (2:26c; 2 Sam. 15:24, 29; 1 Chron. 15:11-15). This generous act of Solomon noted that even though Abiathar "deserve[d] to die, [Solomon would] not put [him] to death now" 2:26c). Therefore, Abiathar got a reprieve from death, but his living out his days depended on his continued behavior before the eyes of the king and his God.

It should also be noted that the removal of Abiathar from being an active priest and replacing him with Zadok as High Priest was in fulfillment of God's word to Eli in 1 Samuel 2:27-36.

Next on Solomon's list of matters to be cleared up of his kingdom was to be fully established was Joab, the commander of the army of Israel (2:28-29). However, when Joab, one of the co-conspirators of the Adonijah coup heard what had happened to Adonijah and to Abiathar the Priest, he knew he was in for trouble. So, he fled to the tent of the LORD and claimed sanctuary by grabbing hold of the horns on the altar (2:28). Solomon was informed about Joab's action, but Solomon resolutely sent his new commander of the troops, Benaiah, to go "strike him down" (2:29). But when Benaiah ordered Joab "to come out [of the tent of the LORD]," Joab refused, saying, "No, I will die here" (30b). The new commander returned to Solomon with the news that Joab refused to give up his position of sanctuary in the tent of the LORD, but Solomon countered with his command, "Do as he says. Strike him down and bury him, and so clear me and my father's house of the guilt of the innocent blood that Joab shed" (31). Obviously, what Joab was aiming to do was to put Solomon in a bad light by making him seem as if he were violating the traditional concept of sanctuary.

Solomon sent Benaiah back to the tent where Joab was claiming sanctuary with orders to do exactly what he had wished. Solomon was more interested in removing the charge of "blood-guiltiness" from his father David's record as well as from him, for this act was of greater significance to Solomon than any charge about violating sanctuary principles. But Solomon did not regard the previous two murders that Joab had committed as being of no consequence; instead, they were matters of conscience and justice had to be served. It is an unsolved problem why David had not cared for this problem based on the same grounds but had left it to be addressed by Solomon.

Solomon Elevates Benaiah as Commander and Zadok as Priest – 2:35-46

Solomon quickly installed Benaiah the son of Jehoida as commander over the army of Israel to replace the former Joab in that position. Likewise, the king moved just as rapidly to replace Abiathar the High Priest with Zadok. It is interesting to note that the descendants of Zadok retained the office of High Priest until 171 B.C.E., when the wicked Antiochus changed the order of succession to the Priest Menelaus. This did not sit well with the Jewish nation as seen for example in the views of the Essenes of Qumran. They waited the replacement of the appointments to the office of Priest back to the Zadokite line, for in their view that line was the only legitimate line of Priests. This view is confirmed by the prophet Ezekiel, who in Ezekiel 44:15-16 pointed to the Zadokites as the only recognized priestly family in those coming eschatological days of the building of the third Temple in the last days.

David had warned Solomon about one more conspirator who had sided with David's son Absalom in an earlier coup; a man named Shimei. David in a magnificent move of generosity had forgiven Shimei of his act of throwing stones and heaving curses at King David when he was fleeing Jerusalem during Absalom's rebellion (2 Sam. 19:18-23). To make sure no trouble would come to the kingdom because of this man, Solomon sent for him and instructed him very carefully, "Build yourself a house in Jerusalem and live there, but do not go anywhere else" (1 Kgs. 2:36). However, "The day you leave and cross the Kidron Valley, you can be sure you will die; your blood will be on your own head" (2:37). Solomon knew he was dealing with a first-class rebel, who if he ever got on the loose, could stir up an enormous amount of trouble for the king and his kingdom. To this proposition Shimei agreed promising he would observe these limits (2:28).

All went well for the first three years (2:39). But then one day, two of Shimei's slaves ran off to Achish, the king of Gath. When Shimei heard that his slaves had fled, he saddled up his donkey and went to Gath, where he retrieved his slaves and brought them back to Jerusalem.

When Solomon was told what Shimei had done, the king called Shimei into his office and asked if he had violated the promise he had made (2:41-42). Never did Shimei think he should have referred this problem to the king before he acted. Instead, he went right ahead on his own to act without anyone's permission. Therefore, the king lectured him, "You know in your heart all the wrong you did to my father David. Now the LORD will repay you for your wrongdoing" (2:44). Solomon concluded that by his taking the action they both had agreed on, not only would he the king be blessed (meaning that the action he was to take was fully justified and injustice of those former days had fully been dealt with), but "David's throne would remain secure before the LORD forever" (2:45). With that, Solomon gave the order to Benaiah, and he struck down Shimei. (2:46). With all those acts accomplished, "The kingdom was now firmly established in Solomon's hands" (2:46c).

Conclusions

1. Solomon did not arrange or employ a counter plot to assure that his throne would be secure for himself. With enormous restraint he waited for the Lord to vindicate his name and his kingdom.

2. Leadership positions are not gained by sheer ambition and movements of self-help, for all promotion to offices of leaders comes directly from God. Unless the Lord builds the house or the dynasty, those who labor on their own will accomplish little more than frustration and trouble.

3. When part of the leadership team backs the wrong horse because they have not sought the wisdom of God in the matter, they are bound for nothing but sorrow in the days to come.

4. When one breaches an oath to God and flaunts the gracious pardon of the one he had previously offended, that person will then face the justice meted out in the oath sworn to.

Questions for Thought and Reflection

1. Do you think Bathsheba really was naïve about Adonijah's request to have Abishag the Shunammite as his wife, or was she just playing along, and in this way alerting Solomon as to what was going on?

2. If Adonijah was aware that his brother Absalom had failed in his attempt to pull off a coup to steal the kingship from his father David, why do you think he thought he could get away with what his brother had failed to pull off? What did he think he had going for him?

3. What might have accounted for King David's hesitancy to take care of some of these offenders of the state, but he instead left that work to Solomon to complete?

4. What other possible means of extradition could Shimei have appealed to without risking his own life by violating his stay in Jerusalem?

Lesson 3

Solomon's Request
for a "Hearing Heart"

1 Kings 3:1-28

This chapter begins with some details in verse 1 that leave us with a question in our minds: Was the "alliance" Solomon made with Pharaoh king of Egypt a positive feature and a sign that Israel was now being held in a place of honor and prestige among the nations? Or was it a sign, hints of the beginning of Solomon's ultimate downfall as this "marriage alliance" with Pharaoh and his daughter was sealed? Scholars have argued this question both ways in the past, but there indeed was a clear prohibition in the Scriptures against intermarriage with unbelievers (Exod. 34:11-16 and Deut. 7:1-5). Certain kinds of diplomacy called for such marriages in Solomon's day to be registered among the better nations. Even though the Biblical proscription was specifically directed against marrying Canaanite women, the principle still held for all other marriages outside the boundaries of the faith of Yahweh. Some add that the mention of Solomon's building his own palace, prior to his building the house of the Lord, was another indication of a set of wrong priorities, i.e. his program ahead of God's program! In fact, Solomon had already married Naamah from the nation of Ammon, as can be determined by the fact that Solomon's son Rehoboam was forty-one years old at the time he came to the throne of David. Since Solomon reigned for forty years, he had already married Naamah the Ammonite before he became King (cf. 1 Kgs. 14:21; 11:42-43), so this new marriage may have been only another sign of his wandering away from the Lord. Thus, we conclude that despite other commendable features in the life of this new king of Israel, some negative tendencies were already appearing. It is hard to read this record any other way!

By the time we come to the end of Solomon's life in 1 Kings 11, there are more evidence of all kinds of foreign alliances and marriages outside of the faith that clearly did contribute to his downfall, so the signs seem to have been there since much earlier in time. Yet all of this was in the face of the fact that I Kings 2 had repeatedly stressed the fact that the kingdom of Solomon had been "firmly established" (1 Kgs. 2:12, 24, 45, 46). Why, then, was it so necessary for Solomon to add these alliances and marriages to further ground and secure his kingdom. Was this not an indication that there was a failure to fully trust God? What more security did Solomon need beyond the fact that God had firmly established his kingdom?

There are three steps Solomon took as he asked and received a wise and hearing heart from God.

I. A Love for the Lord Despite Seeds of a Coming Fall

II. A Dream and a Prayer for Wisdom

III. A Proof That Wisdom Had Been Granted and Approval Granted by the Public

A Love for The Lord Despite Seeds of a Coming Fall – 3:1-3

Why the writer of 1 Kings placed the announcement of Solomon's marriage to Pharaoh's daughter at the beginning of his reign is hard to understand, unless that also was the chronological order of things. It may also have been put there, however, as a secular signal that continued the note that appeared at the end of chapter 2 that "The kingdom was now firmly established in Solomon's hands" (2:46); but that achievement, however, was the work of God. Even so, the full respect shown by Pharaoh king of Egypt to Solomon would have had further confirmation by the esteem Solomon had earned from him and confirmed by the further fact that Pharaoh gave the town of Gezer as a wedding gift to Solomon. The exact identification of the identity of this Pharaoh is not fully known, but it may have been Pharaoh Siamun, the next to last Pharaoh of the twenty-first dynasty, a time when Egyptian influence in the ancient Near East was beginning to fade.

Therefore, despite all our modern rationalization that wants to excuse Solomon, once again the Bible tells it like it is — with warts and all. Here were the seeds of Solomon's downfall, already they were being sown at the very start of his administration. This marriage was meant to seal the political alliance of Israel with Egypt, while it also indicated how important Solomon was now regarded by the nation of Egypt. Previously, the Egyptian Pharaohs had refused to allow their daughters to be married to some of the most powerful foreign kings, but now with Egypt's power declining, Pharaoh Siamun saw that it would be an advantage to ally himself with Solomon, while he also gave his daughter to him in marriage along with the town of Gezer as a wedding gift to Solomon.

As if to confirm that these actions on the king's part were out of line with the rest of his character, verses 2 and 3 also immediately add restrictive adverbs, in v. 2 "however" and "except" in v. 3. The "high places" continued to be a sore point in Israel's behavior before God, for they were the frequent object of the prophet's protest and stern rebuke. Usually they were the places where, by Canaanite custom, Israelites practiced a type of syncretistic worship of the God of Israel and the gods of Canaan. Israel had been carefully instructed that when they came into the land of Canaan, they were to worship at the central sanctuary appointed by God. However, at his point, the house of God had not yet been built. At first, as Israel entered the land of Canaan, the tabernacle had been placed in Shiloh, but when the Philistines captured the Ark of the Covenant, Shiloh lost its significance. Even after the Ark was returned by the Philistines, it remained in the house of Abinadab (1 Sam. 7:1) for a long time, until David removed it to Jerusalem to a tent he had prepared there (2 Sam. 6:17). In between these two events, the Ark was moved to Nob (1 Sam. 21), at which place King Saul massacred the priests stationed there. Then, it appears that the center of worship for the Tabernacle was moved to Gibeon, which is mentioned in connection with Zadok's high priestly ministry, but which ministry was without the presence of the Ark, which presumably had remained in the tent David made for it in Jerusalem (2 Chron. 1:3-5).

Despite all this potential for future Solomonic failures, v. 3 announced that "Solomon showed his love for Yahweh by walking according to the statues of his father David, except he offered sacrifices and burned incense on the high places." This text represents high commendation as well as an important qualification, which is here noted in the word "except." Solomon loved the Lord and chose to walk in the same path that David, his father had taken. Even though Solomon was far from perfect, yet his general attitude and deep desires were focused on following the Lord. Here was a man who was the son of Bathsheba, a son of an adulterous relationship, yet he was forgiven in the grace of God and surprisingly made a candidate for the highest office in the land.

While the qualifying statements in verses 2 and 3 may only have been intended to show that the places of worship were at that time incomplete, they do seem to detract from the otherwise positive statements about Solomon. It is true, of course, that Samuel the prophet brought offerings to various high places (1 Sam. 9:11-25), and that these offerings may have merely supplemented what was offered at the tabernacle. However, when the Temple was built later, all high places were declared illegitimate. It is also true that the text itself says that the offering at these high places was "because a Temple had not yet been built for the Name of the LORD" (2b). Therefore, the qualification was somewhat mitigated.

A Dream And A Prayer For Wisdom – 3:4-15

Solomon began his reign by taking his entire leadership team (2 Chron. 1:2-3) up to Gibeon where he offered a huge sacrifice to the Lord. Gibeon was seven miles to the northwest of Jerusalem, identified with the city of modern El-Jib by the etymological similarity of the names El-Jib and Gibeon, but also by the numerous jar handles with the name of the city inscribed with GBN ("Gibeon") on them, when J. B. Pritchard excavated there around 1960. Since no shrine or altar installation was found at Gibeon, it is conjectured that what was intended was the site of Nabi-Samwil located on a nearby hilltop. Here Solomon offered a thousand burnt offerings to the Lord when he worshiped there (4).

At this site, God appeared to Solomon in a dream during the night, which surely must have indicated to him that God had accepted his burnt offerings. Then God urged him "Ask for whatever you want me to give you" (5b). Therefore, the theme of this section became the word "ask," for the verb occurs eight times (5, 10, 11 [5 times], 13). In response, Solomon prayed what many regard as a remarkable prayer (6-9).

Instead of beginning with his request, Solomon began by briefly reviewing what God had done for their fathers in the past (6-7). Not only was this the real foundation for all prayer, but it focused on the Hebrew word "loving kindness" (*ḥesed*), a word that appears almost 250 times in the Old Testament. It is difficult to express fully this concept in English, for almost 50 English terms have been used to render all that is wrapped up in this term. I think that overall, our word "grace" is the best word to render this important term. Repeatedly, God demonstrated his grace and loving kindnesses to the people and leaders of Israel.

His prayer began with the promises God had given to King David in 2 Samuel 7, but then he went on to the more ancient promises given to Abraham, almost a millennium earlier. Had not the Lord promised that Abraham would have a people too numerous to be counted (Gen. 13:16; 32:12). In fact, that is what God had already delivered. These promises and their fulfillments were evidence that Yahweh had been faithful in his "loving kindnesses," that is it was in his "grace." This type of remembering fosters a depth of gratitude to God and an expectation for God to work on in areas that still lie ahead of us.

However, Solomon is also keenly aware of his own smallness and inexperience for such a huge task. He felt like a "little child" (7b), for he did not know how to carry out the duties that would be expected of him (7c). It is because of these deficiencies that he pled with God to give him a "hearing heart" (literal rendering of the Hebrew). In this case, the "heart" did not mean a part of his anatomy, but here it took in the totality of his intellect, affections and his will. He needed to act favorably in carrying out the welfare of his people (9b). His primary concern was not for his own enhancement; instead, he was concerned for the success of God's people. He needed help from above to rule and discern what was good and right for the people of Israel. If he was to rule over Israel, it would need to be a rule that had their interests and justice uppermost in his mind.

This kind of concern pleased the Lord (10), for Solomon had not put himself first and the most important item in his request, for Solomon did not ask for a long life or for wealth for his own success and profit, nor had he asked for the death of his enemies; no, he wanted instead to have a discernment that would help him administer justice (11c). Therefore, not only did God grant what he had asked for, i.e., "a wise and discerning heart, so that there will never have been any like you, nor will there ever be" (12b), but God would add what he had not asked for: "riches and honor" (13). In fact, God would grant such an abundance of these added benefits that "in [his] lifetime [that he] will have no equal among [any other group of] kings" (13b). The wealth accumulated by historical figures such as the Pharaohs of Egypt, the kings of Assyria, and the rulers of Asia Minor was substantial. Similarly, the wealth provided to Solomon was significant.

All of this was not on an automatic outlay of gifts, for it would also depend on Solomon's walk with God (14). It is not as if God would fail to keep his covenant with David, if Solomon failed to live up to what God expected, for God's promises would remain inviolable to the end regardless of how these kings acted; it was instead a matter of whether Solomon would himself participate and enjoy those same blessings to their fullest. As one in the chosen line of David, he was required to transmit these divine blessings on the next in the Davidic line, but not all of those who were in that Davidic line participated in those blessings. That participation depended on their own personal faith, trust and obedience. Moreover, God would grant to Solomon a long life in addition to all the rest of his promised blessings. Hence the bases for all successful prayer is found first in asking and making our requests made known to God, then in recalling and remembering all God's goodness to us in the past up to that point, and then asking for aid to be given out for the sake of the people of God — all the while acting in a way that is pleasing to him.

Verse 15 noted that Solomon "returned to Jerusalem [and] stood before the ark of the LORD's covenant and sacrificed burnt offerings and fellowship offerings." Unfortunately, some view this text as a later insertion to emphasize the primacy of Jerusalem as the center of worship. But there is no evidence that demands such a conclusion. Solomon may have offered these sacrifices for the convenience of those in different localities, or to show his respect for Jerusalem's status in addition to everything else.

A Proof That Wisdom Had Been Granted and Approval Granted by the Public – 3:16-28

The writer selected a court case in Jerusalem that had been brought by two prostitutes to show that God had indeed given Solomon a "hearing heart" (9). We hear from the accuser what this case was about, for even though some may wonder how the one mother knew what took place, since she by her own testimony was asleep when her baby was switched, she was able to reconstruct the events based on her recognition of the identity of her own baby (21), and thus she could assume what must have taken place while she slept. The case was almost unsolvable, but God had given wisdom to Solomon.

The facts were that the two women both gave birth to each of their babies just three days apart. They both stayed in the same house where they were alone with no others living with them who might have served as witnesses, so this case called for unusual wisdom to solve. The accuser alleged that the other woman's baby died because of being smothered by her mother laying on her baby during the night, for the babies slept in the same bed with both women. When the offending woman discovered what she had accidentally done, she got up in the middle of the night, without the other woman knowing what was going on, and she pilfered the living child from the accuser and replaced in the arms of the unsuspecting sleeping mother the dead baby (19-20). When the accuser awoke the next morning, she found the dead baby at her side, but she unabatedly insisted, "It was not the son I had [given birth to]" (21b). This mother knew her baby and what she had was not her baby.

How was Solomon to decide this case since all the conventional means (e.g., such as witnesses) for making such decisions were not to be had! The desire of the mother of the dead baby was stronger to be a mother to any baby than was her grief and sorrow over the loss of her own child. Now she also envied the mother of the living baby, so with a rapid exchange of the two babies in the pre-dawn light, she was able to satisfy her envy and her maternal instincts by making the transfer of the bodies of the two babies.

Solomon briefly went over the opposing claims of the two mothers (23), then he called for sword to be brought as he issued the order to "Cut the living child in two and give half to one and half to the other" (25). However, this order so alarmed the real mother of the living child that she was overcome by compassion for the life of her child. She instead pled with the king, "Please, my lord, give her the living baby! Don't kill him!" (26b). If the accuser could not find justice, at least she could argue for retaining the life of her baby. (26a). This outburst was the clue Solomon needed; he had indeed smoked out who was the real mother of the baby 927). Give the live baby to the accuser, Solomon concluded. She is the mother of that baby.

When word got out to the public about the verdict the king had offered, "they [all] held the king in awe, because they saw that he had [been given] wisdom from God to administer justice" (28). Solomon had asked God for the ability "to judge" his people (3:9, 11, 28), but here was the evidence that that was exactly what God had given to King Solomon. He had also asked for the ability "to discern" (9, 11, 12) and his discernment in this case was clear to everyone, for his reputation spread like wildfire among the people of Israel and even beyond their borders, as the visit of the Queen of Sheba would later certainly certify.

Conclusions

1. Despite some initial failures at the start of Solomon's reign, God's grace was greater than all Solomon's sin. The story of God's grace begins quite early in Scripture!

2. Solomon showed his love for the Lord by exhibiting a lifestyle that was in most instances pleasing to God.

3. When given a choice to ask for anything he wished for, Solomon chose wisdom and a "hearing/listening heart" above riches, wealth, honor, or victory over his enemies.

4. When God gave Solomon wisdom, it was so awesome that everyone who heard of his use of that wisdom marveled over his powers of judgment and discernment.

Questions for Thought and Reflection

1. What is your estimate of Solomon marriage alliance with the daughter of Pharaoh? Was it an act of disobedience to the word of God?

2. Why is it important to see that our children marry only believers? How is that best secured?

3. What is so important about Solomon's dream coming to him at Gibeon? How can we reconcile God's gift to Solomon in a dream if he was going off the tracks of consistently serving God?

4. Point out the evidence that exists for the divinely gifted discernment to Solomon in the case of the women who each had a baby about the same time, but one of the babies somehow died, yet both were saying the live baby was theirs.

5. Was Solomon's worldly recognition by Pharaoh worth the international prestige considering what it was going to cost him? Can you point out how this might have set him up for future losses in the kingdom of God?

Lesson 4

Solomon's Regime and His Wisdom

I Kings 4:1-34

First Kings 4:1-6 continues the theme of the "wisdom" given to Solomon that was begun in chapter 3 but now is further elaborated on in 4:29-34 and is meant as a wrap up of all the parts of chapter 4. Solomon's economic success was directly rooted in the gift of wisdom granted to him by our Lord. Evidence of Solomon's use of this wisdom can be seen in his roster of high officials and the assignments given to each official on his administrative team (1-6). From there, the text went on to show how this wisdom was worked out in Solomon's tax-collecting apparatus, that provided him with royal revenue (7-19). This was further expanded on in verses 20-28 as more evidence of God's blessing was given in the tally of all the food requirements that were made on Solomon's administration each day in vv. 20-28. All of this was capped off by the theology of Wisdom in this entire chapter.

The picture we are given in 1 Kings 4:1-34 is one of a stunningly high standard of living that depicted a time of peace and prosperity. In fact, two important notices of the great wealth and prosperity in the days of Solomon's reign are found in 4:21 and 24. The first noted that Solomon ruled over "all the kingdoms from the river [i.e., the Euphrates River] to the land of the Philistines [i.e., the Gaza Strip], down as far as the border of Egypt. These countries brought tribute and were Solomon's subjects all his life." Solomon presided over this network in a time of peace, but one that contributed mightily to the wealth and ease that Jerusalem experienced because of this system of taxation. Moreover, the "Pax Solomon," i.e., the peace or Shalom that Solomon imposed, extended over all the kings from the west of the Euphrates River (i.e., "from Tiphsah") down to "Gaza" of the Philistines in the southwest part of Canaan, which today is known as the Gaza Strip. During Solomon's reign, all these kings and lands had "peace on all sides" (24b) and all "lived in safety" (25). This text went on to mention, in this same line of praise, that his government had four thousand stalls for chariot horses and he also had twelve thousand horses" (26). While there is no record of Solomon ever needing to use this extensive mechanized cavalry force, the very fact that he had such military muscle available must have been enough of a deterrent in and of itself to keep the international flow of revenue coming into the city of Jerusalem from taxes and trade.

Later celebrations of Solomon's economic gains can be seen in 1 Kings 9:10-10:29. In these texts, Solomon's reputation for success and prosperity grows as seen by the following: in 1 Kings 9:10-14 where other buildings are built beside the Temple, in 9:15-24 where Solomon used forced labor to make possible these building efforts, in 9:26-28, and in 10:11-12 where Solomon went on to venture in on a project to float a commercial fleet, and in the huge gold inventories Solomon amassed (10:14-25), not to mention his dealing in arms (10:26-29). All this is worth examining in more detail.

There are three proofs that because of the gift of God's wisdom, wealth went from little to an enormous amount.

I.   Wisdom is Seen in the Arrangement of the Royal Administration

II. Wisdom is Seen in the Collection of Taxes and Royal Revenue

III. Wisdom is Seen in the Extent of the Wisdom Granted

Wisdom is Seen in the Arrangement of the Royal Administration – 4:1-6

We are surprised to notice that the main officials in 4:1-6 are the same men who intervened on Solomon's behalf at the time of David's death. Included in this list was first, Azariah, Zadok's son (which in common Hebrew usage of the word "son" was Zadok's grandson, 1 Chron. 6:8-9) as High Priest (2). Zadok appeared to be quite old at the beginning of Solomon's reign, so it was not long before Azariah replaced him as High Priest. He was followed in this list by two secretaries (who were both private secretaries as well as secretaries of state), a "recorder" (who oversaw palace ceremonies and chief of protocol), and the "commander in chief" of the army (3-4), but Benaiah had previously been named to be the commander of David's special guard. Two more priests were noted (4b) and a chief over the twelve district governors (later listed separately, but the district of Judah was for some reason excluded), another priest, who was "a personal advisor to the king" (5b), another who was a superintendent or chief steward over the palace (6a), but whose job gradually increased in importance until he became comparable to the office of an Egyptian vizier, a minister of state, and one who often was empowered to speak for the king.

Finally, the one "in charge of forced labor" or the corves (6b) was Adoniram. Even though this system was by now widely used in the ancient Near East, Samuel had long ago warned (1 Sam. 8:12-17) that the use of such a system would lead to one to the great evils in a monarchy. While in Solomon's time, the heavy weight of this system of taxation was usually borne mainly by foreigners, rather than by Israelite citizens. What taxes were laid on Israel eventually led to such bitterness in Israel that after Solomon died it caused a split and division of the nation into two kingdoms. The assassination of Adoniram, the officer in charge of the forced labor, underscored that point.

Since the same names as were part of Solomon's installation team, whose quick action beat back the potential coup of Absalom, there was continuity from the reign of David to that of his son. Surely, they, above all others, would have been aware of how important it was to plan carefully and to be fully staffed, so the survival of the kingdom was provided for in these transitional times. Thus, there would be no "new faces" in the government, but as already mentioned, a continuation of most of those connected with David's era and administration. Everything was reduced to a manageable system. This was quite a contrast from the loose governmental forms of the era of King Saul. What is even more remarkable is the fact that Solomon here introduces a model of government that he had learned from Egypt, from which the liberated nation of Israel had fled years ago under Moses, which time was not more than four hundred years prior to the present time. It is in Egypt that we find the descriptions of such palace officials as that of scribe, recorder, friend of the king, palace overseer, and head of the forced labor administration. These cabinet posts served the state department and aided the close working of the kingdom of Israel under Solomon.

Wisdom is Seen in the Collection of Taxes and Royal Revenue – 4:7-28

Verses 7-19 lists the twelve districts in Israel (excluding Judah) along with each of their governors, who were each charged with providing one month of goods for the needs of the palace. It was their task to send the revenues needed to sustain Solomon's palace, his court officials, and his household for one month each year. At least two of these district supervisors were Solomon's sons-in-law (11, 15).

The daily provisions (22-25) consisted of "thirty cors of fine flour and sixty cors of meal." A "cor" was a rather large measure of capacity equivalent to a "homer," ("a donkey load"). Though estimates varied quite widely, it ranged somewhere between 48–100 gallons of goods. Kenneth Kitchen estimated that a month's need could be gathered from a crop covering about 424 acres (Kitchen, *Reliability,* p. 133); see also Eugene Merrill (*Kingdom of Priests,* p. 308) broke it down further into 185 bushels of flour and 375 bushels of meal. Others put the amount of the flour needed at 150 – 280 bushels and the meal or course flour between 300 to 560 bushels. Nevertheless, it was a huge goal for most to complete.

In addition to this, there were the daily table needs for 20 pasture-fed cattle, 100 sheep and goats and an assortment of wild game every day. All of this seems to be fantastically high and not at all within the capabilities of the twelve districts of that day, but Kenneth Kitchen is not duly impressed. He reasoned from usages found in the daily and monthly accounts of other ancient Near Eastern palaces, especially those of the third and second millennium and found these figures of Solomon to be within the same range (*Reliability,* p 133). By some estimates, Solomon must have been feeding between 4,000 and 5,000 persons a day off his table. Others set the estimates between 14,000 and 32,000 persons being fed per day!

Beside all of this, there was the need to feed Solomon's large stables of horses, so there were additional quotas of barley and straw that were needed for these chariot horses (28). Recall that Solomon had 12,000 horses and stalls for 4,000 chariot horses (26; cf. parallel in 2 Chron. 9:25). It all seems overwhelming, but such a demand was not over the top for those who had been promised not only wisdom from God, but the blessing of heaven upon all that he did as well.

In trying to get a handle on the extent of the blessing of God on Solomon, one must also include his personal wealth. On two separate occasions, Solomon was given 120 talents of gold, first by King Hiram of Tyre (9:14) and then again by the queen of Sheba (10:10). The total represented by this amount of gold would, if combined, be about nine tons (or 8 metric tons). But the amount of gold that Solomon took in yearly was "666 talents" of gold, which amounted to 25 tons (23 metric; 10:14). These figures so astound many critics of this text that they tend to dismiss it all as fantasy, but again Kenneth Kitchen did not think that such amounts were unusual, for King Metten II of Tyre (c. 730 B.C.E.) paid a tribute of 150 talents of gold to King Tiglath-pileser III of Assyria, while Sargon II (the king who followed Tiglath-pileser III) gave 145 talents of gold to the Babylonian gods as a gift! A way of checking on the reality of such numbers in Israel is to note that, when Pharaoh Shishak invaded Israel after Solomon died c. 925 B.C.E., when he carted off an enormous amount of gold. Shishak's successor in Egypt, Osorkon I, on a long wall inscription (now partially damaged) noted in his first four years of his reign as Pharaoh, he gifted the gods and temples of Egypt with some 383 tons of gold. Such a sum would be equal to almost seventeen years of Solomon's annual gold revenue. There is little doubt that most, if not all, of Osorkon's generosity stemmed from the wealth that his father Shishak had gained from his campaign in Israel and Judah in the days of Solomon's son King Rehoboam. No other monarch of this period in the ancient Near East approaches this scale of spending and back-up reserves as Pharaoh Osorkon I exhibited. The only other monarch who rivaled Solomon in wealth (but who came much later) is Alexander the Great, who took from one city alone, Susa, the Persian city, 1,180 tons of gold. All told, he collected 7,000 tons of gold, which he took back from the Persian Empire! (Kitchen, *Reliability, p*134.)

The joy that Solomon's wisdom and blessing produced is evident in vv. 20-21. Not only had the Abrahamic promise been about a people "as numerous as the sand on the seashore" been fulfilled (4:20a; cf. Gen. 22:17; 32:12), but they were a happy people eating, drinking, and rejoicing (20b). Everyone in Israel sat "under his own vine and fig tree" in security, peace and happiness (25b).

Wisdom is Seen in the Extent of the Wisdom Granted – 4:29-34

Solomon exhibited the wisdom he had received as one who was the embodiment of efficiency and prosperity. The only way to account for Solomon's unprecedented accomplishments was the blessing that came from God.

Of course, a wise ruler is the source for making a joyful people. But it was also because God was fulfilling his covenantal promises he had made earlier to the patriarchs and to David. God had promised that the number of the people would be numerous (Gen. 22:17), and indeed they had become exactly that! They were by now as many as "the sand by the sea." However, God had also promised a place for them in the land formerly occupied by the Canaanites (Gen. 15:18-21), which promise was reconfirmed to them under the Sinai Covenant (Exod. 23:31; Deut. 11:24; Josh. 1:4). A third aspect of God's blessing to his people under Solomon was a time of "peace" (4:23b, 25; 2 Sam. 7:10-11).

It is little wonder, then, that the text is filled with the joy and gladness that comes from God's people. When God's promises are fulfilled and God's people experience them first-hand, it is a matter for rejoicing, happiness, and joy flowing over the entire realm, and the work of the one God who has placed each king at the helm of that nation.

This "wisdom" (Hebrew, hokmah) had both a broad side, as seen in the skill granted for statesmanship and the skill granted for administration (cf. the two craftsmen who worked on the tabernacle, Exod. 31:3), as well as a practical side where this wisdom was applied to life. But at the heart of such wisdom was the concept that God was the author and end of life that was intended to be meaningful and successful. In fact, "The fear of the LORD; that is wisdom" taught Job 28:28. In true wisdom, God gave the ability to see things from God's perspective; it gave a discernment that comes from above and is available for all matters spiritual and moral. It also helps mortals to distinguish between what is good, righteous and helpful versus what is wicked, harmful and evil. Every aspect of human life was included in this gift from God: matters that were intellectual, spiritual, practical, moral, and secular. It embraces our relationship to God as well as our relationship to other persons.

Six times "wisdom" appears in vv. 29, 30, and 34 along with other synonymous terms for wisdom. However, the reader must be careful not to attribute the praise to King Solomon, for the text is clear that God gave this wisdom; Solomon was not a self-made man or a self-made ruler. God granted Solomon exceptional wisdom (30-31). Men were sent to listen to Solomon's wisdom by the kings from all the nations round about Israel (34). The kings of the world had heard of Solomon's wisdom, so they wanted to get first-hand reports of this wisdom for themselves.

The scope of Solomon's gift can be seen in the output that came from his work. For example, "He also spoke 3,000 proverbs and his songs numbered 1,005 (v. 32, or as the LXX probably incorrectly translated it, 5,000 songs!) Moreover, Solomon "described [all sorts of] plant life, from the cedar of Lebanon to the hyssop that grows out of the walls." He taught about animals and birds, reptiles and fish (33).

The extent of this man's wisdom has a range that goes way beyond any of his proverbs or songs. He can move easily from the moral realm to the biological areas of life; he had few, if any areas that he did not explore with joy and fascination. He is an incurable explorer of the whole of God's created realm! In this way, he has gained lots more wisdom by retracing the finger of God in all his handiwork in the natural, moral and aesthetic realms.

Conclusions

1. The glories of Solomon's reign are attributed to the gift of God's wisdom.
2. His wisdom can be seen in the way he organized his government to the way he composed proverbs, songs and studied nature.
3. The extent of his royal splendor was direct evidence of both the ancient promises made to the patriarchs and the new gift of wisdom granted to David's son.
4. The gift of God became an avenue for Solomon to reach out in this time of peace to the kings and nations of other countries who had heard of God's gift of wisdom and who therefore came to test that wisdom for themselves.

Questions for Thought and Reflection

1. What was the mark(s) of God's blessing Solomon and the nation of Israel? Is there also a similarity to what nations look like if God blesses them also? What then is the difference between God's blessing Israel and his blessing on a Gentile nation?
2. If wisdom in the Gentile world is seen primarily in the ability to be successful in a single role or profession, how is wisdom that comes from God the same or different? Does the fear of the Lord factor into this whole equation at all?
3. Why was Solomon's wisdom compared to the wisdom of all the men of the East and the wisdom of Egypt?
4. Why did the nation of Israel enjoy such unmitigated years of peace on all sides during Solomon's reign, yet it never attained any of that kind of extended period of peace after Solomon's day?

Lesson 5

Solomon the Builder of the Temple

1 Kings 5:1 – 8:61

So central and so important was the building and dedication of the Temple to the Solomonic government program and his calling from God that it is spread over five chapters in 1 Kings 5:1-9:9. This was the project that David had wanted to accomplish on his own for God, but he was prevented from doing so by the command of God since he had been a man of war. Nevertheless, the authorization for this project did come in a word originally given at first to David in 2 Samuel 7:13, which was reiterated in both 1 Kings 5:5 and 8:19, thus forming another inclusion beside the bracketing of this material in the two appearances of the Lord to Solomon in Gibeon in the two passages of 1 Kings 3:5 and 9:2 that forms a literary unit by placing these passages together as an inclusion.

It was clear that building the Temple for Yahweh was a goal that had been very much on David's heart and mind (2 Sam. 7:1-17; 1 Chron. 17:1-15). Here was another indication that David was "a man after God's own heart," for David felt it was not right for him to live in a cedar palace while the house of God was still only in a tent. But since God had denied to him this privilege of building the house of God, he nevertheless did all he could to get as much of the materials ready for this project as he could, including some enormous gifts which he contributed from his own reserves (1 Chron. 22 and 29).

Often in the ancient Near East the temple functioned as an instrument of consolidation and sign of the peak of political power for the ruler who was that nation's leader. In the case of Israel, others have seen the Temple as the place which symbolized for Israel her reconciliation, her meeting place, and her place of fellowship with God. The Temple was one-way Israelites made sense of the universe. For many in those times, such construction of a place of worship pointed to the replication of the order in the cosmos, showing there was stability, reliability, and the protection from chaos.

Some point to Psalm 46 as further evidence of the celebration of the benefits from the erection of a nation's house of worship. The Psalm celebrates God's presence in Jerusalem, not just the Temple itself. In fact, the detail mentioned in connection with the building of the temple accords nicely with what we know about the Iron Age culture, yet surprisingly enough most historical minimalists (those who deny the reality and historicity of most events and persons in Israel prior to the seventh or eighth century or even later!) are strangely silent on the data concerning the Temple (apparently since it did not fit their theories). Archaeology has produced a partial parallel to the temple at the Syrian site of Tell Tainat, where a three-chamber design of the remains of a pagan worship center are reminiscent of Solomon's building in which he had: a vestibule (Hebrew, *ulam;* 1 Kgs. 6:3), a Holy Place (Hebrew, *hekel,* 6:17), and a Holy of Holies (Hebrew, *debir,* 6:16). Since Solomon requested help from the Phoenicians in constructing the Temple, it is not strange that his building should replicate what may have been a common Phoenician/Syrian model, for the key craftsmen pointed out in the Bible were, in fact, from Phoenicia. Let us look at this achievement in greater detail.

There are three WAYS Solomon employed in his progress of constructing the Temple.

    I. In the Way Preparation Was Made Before Building of the Temple

    II. In the Way the Building Itself Progressed

    III. In the Way the Building Was Dedicated to the Lord

In the Way Preparation Was Made Before Building of the Temple – 5:1-18

Once Solomon had firmly established his administration and his position as king in Jerusalem, he began laying plans for what would be the major achievement of his reign: the building of the Temple for God and palace complexes for his government. This whole project required a great deal of skill and wisdom in giving oversight to this construction. Here again was another evidence of precisely that very gift of God's unusual grant of the impartation of divine wisdom needed by Solomon to carry out this task. In other countries of the ancient Near East, such an endeavor would be considered a monument to the king's own power and glory, but in this case, Solomon was careful to credit it all to the gifts given to him by the Lord.

Hiram king of Tyre "had always loved David" (literal rendering of 5:1c), so it was natural that Hiram would send an emissary to wish Solomon well. This was but another sign that Solomon was experiencing another benefit from his father's good work of making friends for the government. To these good wishes from Hiram, Solomon responded back with the same kindness as he proposed a new trade agreement between the two countries (3-5). Hiram then gave the orders that his own cedar trees should be felled, therefore, Solomon sent along his own men to work alongside of Hiram's knowledgeable lumberjacks in felling the trees and transporting them down from Phoenicia over coastal waters of the Mediterranean Sea to the shores of Israel (6-7). The trade agreement that Hiram and Solomon worked out was now on a much larger scale than the one that had been worked out between David and Hiram (2 Sam. 5:11; 1 Chron. 22:4). Thus, Hiram kept Solomon supplied with cedar and pine logs, while Solomon reciprocated by sending annually to Hiram 125,000 bushels of wheat for Hiram to feed his own household and another 115,000 gallons of pressed olive oil (5:11). This again demonstrated Solomon's wisdom (5:12b) by his managerial skills, as well as his diplomatic abilities, for the two kings and their nations had remarkable peaceful relations year after year (5:12a).

Solomon raised an enormous labor force of some 30,000 conscripted men from Israel (5:13). In this plan, Solomon was to send 10,000 men to the forests of Lebanon for one month at a time, and then they would return home for two months (5:14). Using this rotation, Solomon had each man work for him for four months and the other eight months those same men would work their own fields at home. In addition to this labor force of 30,000, Solomon had a permanent "slave labor force" (1 Kgs. 9:21) that totaled 70,000 carriers, and another 80,000 stonecutters, who worked in the hills (5:15). The task of the stonecutters was to split the rocks from the living rock in the hills, after which the Israelite and Phoenician craftsmen dressed the stones to size and perfection (5:17-18; 6:7). The resulting "large blocks of quality stones" were formed into the large ashlar blocks, which were typical shapes for this time.

All these ashlars were squared off and cut to size while they were still at the quarry (5:17). Additional stones along with the wooden beams were prepared at "Gebal," i.e., Byblos, Phoenicia (5:18), so the actual construction site of the Temple did not experience any of the typical noise associated with construction, in deference to the holiness of God that would inhabit that place when it was completed. Some will notice that in the separate texts of 1 Kings (5:16 and 9:23) and 2 Chronicles (2:18 and 8:10), the actual number of supervisors does not seem to agree, for they are said to be 3,300 in the Hebrew text of 1 Kings 5:16 (along with a few Greek Septuagint texts agreeing), but in 1 Kings 9:23, they are said to be 550 with the numbers given in 2 Chronicles 2:18 as 3,600 and 250 in 2 Chronicles 8:10. The solution to this apparent mathematical tangle is found in the fact that when the two sets of numbers are added in Kings, they come to 3,300 + 550 = 3,850 and in Chronicles 3,600 + 250 = 3,850, thus the total number of 3,850 agrees in all instances! Apparently, the difference arose from a different method of classification of the workers. Chronicles distinguished the Canaanite overseers (3,600) from the Israelite overseers (250), while Kings distinguished the 3,300 lower overseers from the 550 higher overseers. This last group of 550 was divided between 250 Israelite overseers and 300 Canaanite Overseers (5:16).

In the Way the Building Itself Progressed – 6:1-7:51

In the fourth year of Solomon's reign (ca 967/966 B.C.E. according to Thiele's dating), and 480 years since the Israelites were led out of the land of Egypt in 1446 B.C.E. (6:1), construction began on the "house of Yahweh" (6:1b). It often happened in the ancient Near East that major building events were frequently tied to some memorable national happening, as was true of this project as well: in Israel's case it was a celebration of Yahweh's redemption of the people from the land of Egypt. Most critical scholars do not take these numbers literally, which in approximate terms, places the building of the Temple somewhere halfway between the exodus and the exile! But since the Mesopotamian kings gave real and exact figures in the similar circumstances, there is no reason to doubt that the same use of numbers was being observed here.

The general dimensions of the Temple were given in 1 Kings 6:2-10: sixty cubits long by twenty cubits wide. Since the cubit was normally about eighteen inches in length, it was some 90 feet long x 30 feet wide x 45 feet high, with a porch 15 feet long and 30 feet wide; the Temple, therefore, was exactly twice the size of the tabernacle. Also, the site of the Temple was "on Mount Moriah," where the Lord appeared to David on the threshing floor of Araunah the Jebusite (2 Chron. 3:1), as well as the earlier site of the aborted sacrifice of Isaac by Abraham (Gen. 22:2). Moriah would remain a memorable site in the minds of all Israel.

The three chambered Temple had a vestibule (i.e., a porch), a holy place (i.e., the main hall), and a most holy place with "clerestory windows" on the side walls (6:5). The exact nature of these windows is unknown, for they may have been slatted, latticed, or ones that were narrower on the outside than on the inside. Outside the walls of the Temple, surrounding it on three sides, Solomon built a triple-tiered structure of an unspecified number of rooms, whose walls decreased in thickness by one cubit as each of the three floors was placed above the other 6:10).

The writer of 1 Kings spent a good deal more time describing the interior portion of the Temple (14-38), as compared to the exterior (2-10). Both the main hall and the inner sanctum were paneled with cedar (15-18), but they were both overlaid with "pure gold," as was the Temple floor, the huge cherubim in the inner sanctuary, the olive wood doors to the entrances to the main hall and the inner sanctuary, all of which components were coated with "gold" – a word that appears eleven times in this context: (20, 21 [3 times], 22 [2 times], 28, 30, 32 [2 times], and 35).

Why should the writer put so much emphasis on this gold overlay? Solomon and Israel did not consider this gold overlay a waste or an extravagance that could have been avoided. Instead, they saw it as a godly extravagance that was commensurate with the splendor and glory of the Lord God himself. However, the magnificence of the building was not the entirety of the calling God was giving to Solomon and Israel. In 1 Kings 6:11-12, The Lord himself reinforced the real priority he sought by noting, even while the Temple was under construction, there was a lifestyle of faith and belief in the Lord and obedience to all that the Lord of Temple had commanded Solomon to do. God did indeed communicate the mundane facts about the sheer physical proportions of the Temple, but none of this was to be put as a substitute for obeying the word he had given to them, nor was it a substitute for the promises he had given to their father David (6:13).

In the Way the Building Was Dedicated to the Lord – 8:1-61

Solomon assembled all the elders of Israel, as well as the heads of the tribes and families, on the dedication of the Temple. To start this solemn service, priority would be given to the placement of the Ark of the Covenant in the Temple (8:1). No longer would the Ark be housed in temporary quarters of a tent; it would have a permanent home now. In vv. 1-9, the Ark is mentioned eight times, but central to its frequent mention is the fact in v. 9 that there "was nothing in the Ark except the two stone tablets that Moses had placed there at Horeb [Sinai]," for that was the reason why the Ark was called "the Ark of the Covenant of the LORD" as well as the "Ark of the Testimony." Here was the heart of the matter for the Temple: it was the Ark of the Covenant.

The setting for this event was the month of "Ethanim" (A Canaanite name meaning "perennial," marking the onset of the fall, or the "early rain"), later this month was known as "Tishri," meaning "beginning" of the year, the seventh month, equivalent to our September-October. The "festival" referred to here was the Feast of Tabernacles, the Ingathering Festival of the harvest (Lev. 23:33-43), which also recalled Israel's journey through the wilderness. But now that God had given them "rest" (Deut. 12:8-11), the end of that wandering had come! Some have noticed that 1 Kings 6:38 has the completion of the Temple in the "eighth month," thereby supplying us with a notice of a time lapse between the completion and the dedication of the Temple. Therefore, Solomon must have deliberately waited eleven months for the official dedication of the Temple, because it would be symbolically important to connect it with the fulfillment of God's promises at the time of the Feast of Tabernacles or the Feast of Booths. It is this same Feast that in the future will be the one that is mandatory for all Gentiles from all the nations to attend, along with Israel in the Messianic age (Zech. 14:16-21). Moreover, the completion of the Temple fulfilled Moses' prophecy in Exodus 15:17 and in Deuteronomy 31:10-11, wherein God made provision for the renewal of the covenant every seven years at this same time. While such a renewal is not mentioned in this text, or at this time, the mention of the two tablets of the law certainly pointed to the need for Solomon and Israel to keep the word of God as the real source of their personal and national renewal in their hearts and minds.

Just as it happened when the Ark had been placed in the Mosaic Tabernacle (Exod. 40:34-35), so it happened once again: the cloud of the glory of God descended and filled the Temple (8:10). This glory cloud was the visible manifestation of the presence of God, which the Rabbinic scholars designated "the Shekinah glory" ("Shekinah" comes from the Hebrew word *shakan*, meaning "to dwell"). This cloud so filled the whole Temple that the priests had to withdraw from the Holy Place (10a). The Hebrew word for "cloud" in v. 12 is *'arapel,* "thick cloud," which is the same word found in Exod. 19:9; 20:21. Thus, while the Shekinah glory signified God's presence in the world of mortals, the word for "cloud" in v. 12 spoke of God's hiddenness, for it was a "thick, dark cloud." Accordingly, God can be both apprehended (versus his being comprehended in a complete and exhaustive knowledge of his person), yet he in his majesty and person is both inapproachable and at times hidden while he also can and does reveal himself.

Solomon turned from speaking to Yahweh (12) to bless all the people gathered there before him. His blessing began and ended with praise to God for delivering his people out of Egypt (16, 21). The promise of Exodus 15:17 had now been fulfilled.

The content of Solomon's prayer of dedication (23-53) focused on the theme that since God had been pleased to honor his promises to Israel up to that point, would he not continue to be faithful to his promises: first in continuing the line of David (23-26), secondly in accepting the prayers of his people (29), and thirdly in granting forgiveness (30). As Solomon prayed in front of the whole assembly of Israel, he stood on a four-and-a-half-foot high bronze platform (2 Chron. 6:13; 1 Kgs. 8:22). In this act, he stood as the representative of all the people as he offered one of the great prayers of Scripture.

Solomon began his prayer by stating with joy that "There is no God like you in heaven above or on earth" (23a). Our Lord had kept his covenant of love with all his servants who had walked wholeheartedly in his way (23b). All that Yahweh had promised David had also been kept (24). No wonder, then, that God was praised as an incomparably great God. Moreover, the fact that this "God would really dwell on earth," (27) was mind boggling enough, for "even the highest heaven [could] not contain [him]" (27b), much less could a Temple Solomon had built be thought of as containing him! However, despite this incongruity, Solomon dared to make his prayer and request known toward this newly built Temple raised to the glory of this same God who had promised that "My Name [meaning in this case his presence] shall be there" in this Temple (29b). The transcendence of God did not overrule his intimacy or his immanency, for the uncontainable God would nevertheless also be just as accessible as he had shown himself to be in the past.

Solomon proceeded to make seven specific requests of God in vv. 31-53. The first request was a case where no witnesses were available and only an oath was taken before the Lord in a court situation (31-32; Exod. 22:6-12; Lev. 6:1-5). Would God please, in this sort of case, judge the guilty party and thereby attest to the truth of the claim of the innocent party's oath before him? In this way Yahweh would show he honored the altar of the Solomon's Temple just as he had honored the altar of the tabernacle.

The second request was a prayer for forgiveness after Israel had been defeated by an enemy (33-34; cf. Lev. 26:17; Deut. 28:25). The conditions for Israel's restoration as God's people were these: they must turn back to God (repenting), they must confess God's name, and they must make prayer in the house of God. Would God then forgive them?

The third request concerned the drought brought on the land by the sin of the people (35-36; cf. Lev. 26:19; Deut. 28:23). If God did not send the fall and spring rains, the crops would fail. The solution for this crisis, once again, was to pray towards God's house, to confess their sin, and to turn away from those sins (35c). Solomon added to this request that God would teach his people the right way to live so the land he had given to them for an inheritance after they had repented and received the rain they needed (36c).

In Solomon's fourth request he presented a collage of issues, such as: times when the people would experience famine, various kinds of plagues, pestilence, blight and mildew, invasions of locusts and grasshoppers, attacks from besieging enemies, and sickness among the people (37-40; cf. Lev. 26:16, 19-26; Deut. 28:21-23, 38-39, 58-61). In this, he knew well that God was calling Israel once again for repentance and a turning back to himself. The hope was that God's people would live in the "fear" of the Lord (40). This "fear" would be a theme taught and uplifted in the wisdom books.

Solomon's fifth request acknowledged that God would also be working among the Gentiles so that they too might come to know and love the Lord, therefore this king of Israel prayed that foreigners would come to Yahweh as well as Israelites (41-43). This was an evangelistic note and an exercise of missions in the Old Testament.

His sixth request (44-45) was for those times when Israelites would be off fighting in other lands where there was no access to the Temple on that foreign soil. They were to pray to the Lord and toward the city of Jerusalem where the Temple resided. But note the order and priority; it was first to pray to the Lord and only then toward the city, for it was the Lord who answered their prayers, not the Temple or any forms of ritual.

The last of the calamities that Solomon prayed for was the situation where, because of their sin, they were taken captive into a foreign land and exiled from the land of Israel (46-51; cf. Lev. 26:27-39; Deut. 28: 36-37, 41-68). However, just as God had provided hope in Leviticus 26:40-45 and Deuteronomy 30:1-10, so even after such a massive deportation of most of the nation, God would use this calamity to bring Israel back to an awareness of her sin so they she would be forgiven and restored to her land.

The conclusion to this marvelous, believing, intercessory prayer by King Solomon comes in vv. 52-53. Even though he mentioned the Temple all through his prayer, his main concern was for God's continued faithfulness in answering the peoples' prayers in the future. In 2

Chronicles 7:1-3 we find the divine response of approval to the Temple he had built and to Solomon's prayer: it was this: "fire" came down from heaven and consumed the burnt offering. Hence, the Lord accepted both the Temple of God and the prayer of dedication!

When Solomon had finished his dedicatory prayer, he and all Israel rejoiced as they celebrated the Feast of Tabernacles/Booths. As the people left for home after the seven days of festivity, they rejoiced in the favor and blessing of God that had allowed them to now see an established resting place for the house of God and a center for worship in the land after they had gone so long a time without such a place after Shiloh was destroyed sometime around 1050 B.C.E.

Conclusions

1. The building of the Temple by Solomon was another evidence of the gift of God's wisdom. The wisdom and ability of skills of craftsmanship were all given by God.

2. The work on the Temple commenced on the 480th anniversary of Israel's freedom from Egypt and the fourth year of Solomon's reign. Thus, the building recalled Israel's greatest deliverance from the earth's mightiest monarch of that day.

3. The Temple plans showed that God's plans included both the plans for the physical/external world (in the external dimensions of the Temple) as well as the spiritual/internal realm (the heart relationship to God and others).

4. Solomon's view of the greatness of God included his incomparability, immensity, and transcendence along with his intimacy, immanency and faithfulness.

Questions for Thought and Reflection

1. Why does God constantly refer to his deliverance of Israel from Egypt and memorialize that 1447 B.C.E. event by dedicating the Temple on the 490th annual anniversary of that event?

2. If God called for a separation from the world by believers, why does he allow a covenantal relationship with the king and people of Phoenicia in building the Temple?

3. When Solomon dedicated the Temple, he concluded his prayer with the famous verse in 2 Chronicles 7:14 about the possibility of the people and nation being restored to him if they would humble themselves, seek his face, pray and turn from their wicked ways. Is that promise still in effect today and if so, why?

4. What were the seven situations that Solomon included in his prayer of dedication and how applicable are these same or similar conditions applicable to the lives of nations and peoples today.

Lesson 6

Solomon and Israel as a Light to the Nations

1 Kings 9:1-10:29

According to 1 Kings 6:38, it had taken seven years to complete the building of the Temple, therefore what Solomon had begun in the fourth year of his reign he finished in his eleventh year. The work on his palace, however, added another thirteen years to that original project (1 Kgs. 7:1), which meant that he was now twenty–four years into his reign, twenty of which had been spent in constructing the Temple and his palace (1 Kgs. 9:10). Solomon also had fortified and beautified the towns of Jerusalem, Hazor, Megiddo, and Gezer (9:15-19) as part of his many construction projects.

Some view the fact that it took Solomon almost as twice as long to build his palace complex as it did to build the Temple, (13 years for the palace complex compared to 7 years for the Temple) as an indication of poor priorities and emphases on his part, but Scripture did not condemn Solomon as some modern critics have for this disparity in time allocation for each project. The extended time on the palace complex may well have been because there were at least some five buildings associated with the total palace complex. Moreover, the Temple was almost completely gold coated inside, thereby easing the time required for detailed architectural work.

In addition to Solomon's building the palace itself, there was the "Palace of the Forest of Lebanon" (7:2-5), so named because of its cedar construction, measuring 150 feet long, 75 feet wide and 45 feet high, in which the 300 shields of gold were stored for military usage. Isaiah 22:8 called this building the "Palace of the Forest," which served both for ceremonial occasions and as an armory for these weapons. Then there was the "colonnade" (7:6), which served either as a porticoed entry hall, or as a waiting room for those awaiting their hearings in the Hall of Justice. The Hall of Justice (7:7) itself was where Solomon's throne or royal audience chamber was located, as the king heard cases and meted out justice that lesser officials were unable to handle. The throne itself was described in 1 Kings 10:18-20); it too was fabulous and almost beyond description. Finally, Solomon also made a private residence for Pharaoh's daughter (7:8b). All this work exhibited the typical Phoenician construction style in which there were three layers of stone and one layer of cedar beams (7:12), which also was the same style represented in the Solomonic gate at Megiddo.

But Solomon was now at a crossroads spiritually, for after all these years of being occupied with the business of state and being concerned with matters of one construction project after another, he seems now to have faced somewhat of a letdown in his busyness and purpose in life. This is later confirmed in 1 Kings 11:4, where it was noted that as Solomon grew older, his many wives began to turn his heart away from Yahweh and towards other foreign gods. This happened to this monarch even though God had already appeared to him twice (at Gibeon in 1 Kgs. 3:5 and again at Gibeon when he finished building the Temple and the royal palace in 1 Kgs. 9:1). It is not clear why God had waited to appear to Solomon once again some thirteen years after the Temple was finished, but his message and approval of all Solomon had done by the time of their dedication was clear enough (9:3-9). However, God had in fact responded earlier, for it was immediately at the dedication of the Temple when he had appeared in the glory cloud (8:10-12) and when he sent fire from heaven to consume the sacrifices (2 Chron. 7:1-7) at that earlier time to show his approval of what had been accomplished. So, it was not as if Solomon had been left with no indication from God whether he had approved of the Temple project at the time of its completion. But let us look at the whole context for the message from God in an expository style.

There are four indications that Solomon was to act as a light to all the nations of the world with the light of the Gospel.

I. By Receiving the Promised Blessing and the Warning of God

II. By Demonstrating Wisdom in the Affairs of Government

III. By Answering the Hard Questions Posed to Him

IV. By Receiving the Confirmation of the King's Wisdom from the Narrator

By Receiving the Promised Blessing and a Warning – 9:1-9

Even though this second epiphany of the Lord came thirteen years after the completion of the Temple, the Lord apparently wanted to emphasize the fact that he had heard Solomon's prayer, and he had consecrated that Temple by placing his "Name" there forever. Therefore, God's "eyes" and his "heart" would always be there (9:2-3) in that Temple.

The Lord went on to once again remind Solomon and the people of the fact that what the Lord wanted from their Temple worship was not just routine ritual, but evidence of "integrity of heart and uprightness" (4). If this king and his sons who succeeded him would be faithful and obedient to God's word, then God would establish their royal thrones as he had established David's throne (5). But if Solomon and his line of descendants turned away from God, then God would: (1) "cut off" (Hebrew, *karat,* "to cut") Israel from the land he had given to them (7a), (2) reject this Temple he had consecrated and in which he had placed his divine name (7b), and (3) make them a "byword (Hebrew *mashal,* meaning a "proverb"), and an "object of ridicule" (Hebrew *sheninah,* related to the word for "tooth," *shen, or shanan,* "to make sharp", cf. Ps 64:3, "they sharpen their tongues like swords") among all people" (7c). In this later case, so drastic would be the action of the judgment of God against this Temple that all the people who passed by the destroyed residue of the Temple would be "appalled" and would scoff and say, "Why has the LORD done such a thing to this land and to this Temple?" (8b). And the people themselves would answer, it was "because they have forsaken the LORD their God, who brought their fathers out of Egypt, and have embraced other gods, worshiping and serving them – that is why the LORD brought all this disaster on them" (9).

By Demonstrating Wisdom in the Affairs of Government- 9:10-25

This section of the text is a miscellaneous collection about the on-going business of the work of Solomon as the head of the nation, placed between two theological statements found in 1 Kings 9:1-9 and 11:1-13. The first item came from Solomon's trade arrangement with Hiram, king of Tyre in 9:10-14. Originally Solomon had promised to give to Hiram wheat and oil in return for the timber and expertise he had sent to him (5:9,

11), but in this piece Solomon also ceded to Hiram twenty border towns, perhaps indicating that Solomon ran up more debt in lumber and Phoenician workmen skills than he could pay for with foodstuffs. Some think that Solomon bested Hiram in a sort of wheeler-dealer trade, in which Solomon used a very sharp pencil and sort of cheated him by giving him towns that were not worth much, because Hiram complained, "What kind of towns are these you have given me, my brother?" (13). That is why Hiram called them "the land of Cabul" (13b), which understands Cabul as taken from the Hebrew *ka,* meaning "as" and *bal,* meaning "nothing," i.e., a sort of "Zerosville." However, Septuagint read the "K" as a "g" for Hebrew *gebul and* placed the meaning instead as "border" towns! Another view, however, takes these towns as being around the town of "Cabul" (cf. Josh. 19:27), which was in the territory of the tribe of Asher, near the border of Tyre. Nevertheless, Hiram was not too pleased with the gift or the trade agreement. Was this another case of Solomon's wisdom, or did it reflect poorly on this otherwise pious Temple-builder? It is difficult to say based on the evidence we have here.

Another vignette that gives us insight into Solomon's government was his use of the "slave labor force" (9:15-23) that came from all of the Amorites, Hittites, Perizzites, Hivites, and Jebusites, who were descendants of the Canaanites, who had inhabited the land of Canaan, but whom the Israelites "had not exterminated" (20-21) as they had been told to do. These were people from the nations who had been subjected to Israel's invasion, and for whom God had given the order that they were to be exterminated.

However, the usual bleeding-heart-liberal again protests that this is but another evidence of how oppressive Solomon's reign was. But the writer of 1 Kings did not come to the same conclusion, for he saw it as both an evidence of the former generations failure to carry out the will of God long time ago in removing all these people from the land, and as further evidence of Solomon's wise ability to achieve a grandiose plan that allowed him to excel in his preparation for defense of his land and in all of his economic policies. This slave labor force made it possible for Solomon to avoid depending on Israelites for such hard labor, but instead to use Israelites exclusively as his soldiers, his government officials, his officers, his captains, and as commanders of his chariots and charioteers. (22). No Israelite was reduced to the status of a slave.

To further show how enterprising Solomon was in the world of international competition (9:24-28), the writer cited his alliance to the Pharaoh of Egypt by a marriage alliance (24; cf. 9:16; 11:1-2). Later the text will reflect negatively on this marriage (11:1-2), but after pharaoh's daughter left the palace in Jerusalem, Solomon showed more of his wisdom by his work of the "supporting terraces," on what was called "Millo." This structure seems to be in or at the City of David in Jerusalem.

This king also saw that the three annual festivals were kept on a regular basis (25; cf. Exod. 23:14-17). By this means Solomon "fulfilled the Temple obligations" (25c), as set forth in the Mosaic Law. Under his rule, thus far, orthodoxy was alive and well: he obeyed what the word of God taught and instructed.

One other evidence of Solomon's wisdom can be seen in his involvement in shipping and commerce (26-28). Once again, it was Hiram who sent his men to serve in the fleet with the men of Israel, for Hiram's men knew the sea and they knew how to sail on those seas with their navigational skills. As a result, they sailed to Ophir and were able to bring back what amounted to 16 tons of gold to the city south of the Arabah called Ezion-Geber, near Elath on the Red Sea. Ophir as a real site can now be confirmed by an ostracon shipping receipt found near Tell Aviv and dated to the 8th century B.C.E. It read: "Gold of Ophir to Beth Horon, shekels thirty."

By Answering the Hard Questions Posed to Him – 10:1-13

To show the obvious blessing God had bestowed on Solomon, the writer of this text chose to cite the visit of the Queen of Sheba to illustrate how far distant his reputation had spread. "Sheba" is located by most in Southern Arabia, present-day Yemen, over 1,000 miles south of Jerusalem. The first letter in her name, Hebrew *shin,* has a "sh" sound, but that was equivalent in South Arabic to the letter "s," referring to a people known as the Sabeans. This queen had heard of Solomon's widespread "fame," but she did not believe what she had heard at first.

She came "to test him with hard questions" (Hebrew, *hidot,* usually translated as "riddles"), which were sorts of enigmatic questions that embodied deeper philosophical, practical, or theological truth. This was a small part of delegations that were coming from all the nations to listen to Solomon's wisdom (1 Kgs. 4:34). In this manner, God was using Solomon to be a light to all the nations, as he had wanted the nation of Israel to function. Therefore, it must be carefully noted that the goal was also to hear about Solomon's "relationship to the Name of the LORD" (10:1). This was no doubt but a foretaste of the future flow of the nations to Zion (Isa. 2:2-5). Genesis 12:3b had promised that Abraham's "Seed" would be the source for blessing all the nations of the earth.

The queen herself was a great lady who came with a large retinue, loaded with all sorts of goods, meant probably to indicate to Solomon the large extent of her own wealth and success. Her camel caravan carried "spices, large quantities of gold and precious stones" (10:2b). She was able to talk with Solomon "about all that she had on her mind" (10:2c). But Solomon was equal to her inquiries; there was nothing too hard for the king to explain to her (3).

However, despite her elaborate show of wealth, when she saw all the wisdom of Solomon, his palace, the amount and quantity of food on his table, and the number of officials and attending servants with their robes, his cupbearers, and the number of burnt offerings at the Temple, the whole thing took her breath away (4-7).

The Queen of Sheba was not an isolated narrative, but a theme that would be repeated over and over again in the experience of Israel as such blessing was also observed in the lives of: Melchizedek (Gen. 14:18-20), the Hittites (Gen. 23:6), Pharaoh's magicians (Exod. 8:15, the Egyptians (9:20), Jethro (18:9-10), Balaam (Num. 23-24), Rahab (Josh. 2:9-12), Ruth (Ruth 1:16-17), and Naaman (2 Kgs. 5:15). So, this Gentile woman also declared, "How happy/blessed your men must be! How happy/blessed your officials, who continually stand before you and hear your wisdom!" (8). She concluded this paean of praise in verse 9 by saying "Praise be to Yahweh your God, who has delighted in you and placed you on the throne of Israel." She continued: "Because of Yahweh's eternal love for Israel, he has made you king, to maintain justice and righteousness" (9).

The Queen of Sheba gave Solomon four and one-half tons of gold, large amounts of spices and precious stones as a gift (10). Never had the land of Israel seen so many spices as those the queen had brought with her.

But all this largess from the queen caused the writer of this text to add another source for the wealth that was flowing into the nation of Israel: Solomon's joint maritime venture with Hiram was providing another rich source of wealth. Special stress seems to be placed on the precious wood, almug wood, from which Solomon made supports for the Temple and the royal palace along with using it to make harps and lyres for musical instruments (11-12). The identity of this almug wood is not known today, but it seems to be a type of sandalwood or a type of hard reddish-brown wood. It was used at Ugarit (Ras Shamra, Syria), as well at Alalakh, Syria in the fashioning of fine furniture.

Solomon gave the queen all she asked for (13), which may have included some trade agreements since the overland camel routes may have been affected by Solomon and Hiram's maritime ships plying in the Red Sea and perhaps in the Indian Ocean. Ethiopic tradition, however, claims that she wanted Solomon to give her a child. Tradition in that country says she did bear a son, which in turn perpetuated the Abyssinian line. There are no known facts that can substantiate this claim, however.

By Receiving the Confirmation of the King's Wisdom from the Narrator – 10:14-29

Some may doubt such high figures for the wealth of Solomon, but as if to show that it is valid, the narrator represented the amount of gold received on an annual basis as 25 tons. This amount did not include an unspecified amount of revenue that came from merchants and traders from all the Arabian kings and governors of the land (14), who apparently traveled through the land of Israel, and had to pay tariff for the privilege. The "Arabian Kings" were no doubt tribal chiefs who lived in the desert area, which was to the south and east of Israel.

Another indication of Solomon's wealth could be seen in his ceremonial shields that he kept in the Palace of the Forest of Lebanon (16-17). These shields were made of wood or basket-work and covered with gold rather than leather, with the larger shields made in an oval or rectangular shape that could protect the whole body of soldiers in the heavy-armed infantry, each weighing seven and a half pounds, while the smaller shields were carried by the archers and weighted only three and a half pounds. The fact that the book of Kings claimed the large shields had "600" as the unspecified unit of weight while Chronicles read "300," also without specifying the unit of weight, can be shown to agree when it is understood that the Temple "shekel" was one half the weight of the ordinary shekel. The *beka*, a "split shekel," i.e., one half the weight of the ordinary shekel would have reduced what one reported as 600 to 300 in another writer.

Even more impressive and imposing in its structure was the throne of Solomon (18-21). Most think it was made of an understructure of wood and then was inlaid with ivory, but where there was no ivory, it was overlaid with gold. This throne also had six steps with a lion on each step, making a total of twelve lions. The back of the throne had a "rounded top," which seemed similar to the throne of King Ahirma of Byblos and was depicted on his sarcophagus wherein the top of the throne is folded over the back and down in the shape of an inverted U. The throne's armrests were likewise flanked by lions on each side to match the lions on the six steps leading up to the throne.

Add to this the fact that the king's goblets were also gold as were all the household articles in the Palace, for nothing was made of silver, since silver was thought to be of little value in Solomon's day (21) compared to gold. Solomon also had a "fleet of trading ships," or they can also be translated as "ships of Tarshish" (22). The original location of Tarshish has not been firmly identified, but it is generally agreed that it lay somewhere in the western Mediterranean, possibly in Sardinia or Spain. These ships would be gone once every three years, but would come back carrying "gold, silver and ivory, apes and baboons," or some rendered the last item as "peacocks." Some conjecture that the ships, docked in Ezion Geber, used that site as storehouses for all they obtained in trade, but others thought that refined metals were used in exchange for these exotic imports to Israel.

In a statement corresponding to I Kings 4:29-34, the fabulous riches of Solomon became one of the bases for "the whole world [seeking] an audience with Solomon to hear the wisdom God had put in his heart" (23-24). That wisdom included all things sacred and secular, therefore in this way the truth of the gospel was getting out to the whole world and to all its rulers! In this instance, the truth of what God had given to Solomon outstripped the rumors of his success.

One final note on the power and accumulated wealth of Solomon can be found in vv. 26-29: Solomon accumulated 1400 chariots and 12,000 horses, which he kept in chariot cities (26). Typically, according to texts from Ugarit, Ras Shamra, three horses made up a chariot team: a pair and a lead horse. Other horses would be studhorses, or ones in training to replace the chariot teams when they needed to be replenished. But this large collection of horses reminds us of another prohibition in Deuteronomy 17:16-17, where the future king must not acquire large numbers of horses, not to mention the prohibition on taking numerous wives for himself or amassing great quantities of gold! The problem with each of these violations was that they engendered a trust in man rather than a trust in God.

Solomon's horses were imported from Egypt, from "Cue," which can now be identified with Cilicia from the ZKR inscription from Syria in the eighth or ninth century B.C.E. But such trade in horses with these two countries may also have involved Solomon in trade agreements and diplomatic relationships that likewise compromised his testimony. In the eighth century B.C.E. the prophet Isaiah had warned about going to Egypt for help and of relying on her horses and chariots for Israel's defense (Isa. 31:1-3). It is true, of course, that all this wealth came from God, as he had promised, but the gift of God could also become the test from God if one started to pride oneself on what had been accumulated and valued the gift more than one prized God himself!

Conclusions

1. Despite how splendid the Temple was, its fame and importance came by far from the fact that God had placed his Name and presence there.

2. The appearance of God on this second occasion emphasized that the "integrity of heart" and "uprightness" in life was the center of real worship of God.

3. With the prestige that came from the gift of God's wisdom came the challenge to be a light to all the nations as well.

4. God's gifts may bring fame and fortune, but they can just as well bring disaster and decline in spirituality if the gift becomes more important than the Giver.

Questions for Thought and Reflection

1. What do you think we can learn about the practice and principles of worship from this section on the building of the Temple? Should these chapters serve as a model congregation's present search for a theology of worship, or should our day be totally different?

2. What rules, if any, were in force about the use of images, pictures, and representations to be used in the Temple construction and why was this limitation required of Israel? To what degree should such a limitation be a part of our constructing congregational buildings today?

3. If Israel was also called to be a light to the nations, how was this nation to do this? Would it be a method that is totally different from missions programs today?

4. Was the fabulous amount of silver and gold spent on the Temple totally beyond the limits of what God would accept as acceptable in his sight? What financial limits do you think modern congregational buildings should have placed on them by building committees?

5. Was the employment of a foreigner as the chief architect on the Temple an example of stepping beyond the limits of being separate from the world?

Lesson 7

Solomon's Heart Turns Away from God

I Kings 11:1-43

By the time we reach this chapter in Solomon's later years, we have come a long way from where he began early in his life, for in 1 Kings 3:3, "Solomon showed his love for the LORD by walking according to the statutes of his father David." By this time in his life, what had once been a fervent love for the Lord and an obedient walk with the Lord, it was now diverted into a love for his foreign and pagan wives. Solomon must have forgotten all about the promise the Lord had made to him to bless him with all his gifts if he would remain faithful to all that God had called to be and to do.

But when Solomon "grew old" (11:4), his love changed from one of loving God to loving foreign wives who came from Egypt, Moab, Ammon, Edom, Sidon and from the land of the Hittites. His present compromising stand, unfortunately, would be transmitted to others in Israel, as they too began to follow his example in the years that followed. It was not as if Solomon and Israel had not been warned, any less than we in our generation have been warned of the dangers of departing from the Lord. All the way back to the times of Moses, the Scriptural teaching had been made very clear and forthright to all who would listen. For example, Deuteronomy 17:16-17 states that

> The king, moreover, must not acquire great number of horses for himself or make the people return to Egypt to get more of them, for the LORD has told you, 'You are not to go back that way again.' 17. He must not take many wives, or his heart will be led astray. He must not accumulate large amounts of silver and gold.

Deuteronomy 7:1-4 had warned of the same issues:

> When the LORD your God brings you into the land you are entering to possess and drives out before you many nations – the Hittites, Girgashites, Amorites, Canaanites, Perizzites, Hivites, and Jebusites, seven nations larger and stronger than you 2. and when the LORD your

> God has delivered them over to you and you have defeated them, then you must destroy them totally. Make no treaty with them and show them no mercy. 3. Do not intermarry with them. Do not give your daughters to their sons or take their daughters for your sons, 4. for they will turn your sons away from following me to serve other gods, and the LORD's anger will burn against you and will quickly destroy you.

This is almost a repeat of Exodus 34:11-16.

> Obey what I command you today. I will drive out before you the Amorites, Canaanites, Hittites, Perizzites, Hivites and Jebusites. 12. Be careful not to make a treaty with those who live in the land where you are going, or they will be a snare among you. 13. Break down their altars, smash their sacred stones and cut down their Asherah poles. 14. Do not worship any other god, for the LORD, whose name is Jealous, is a jealous God. 15. Be careful not to make a treaty with those who live in the land; for when they prostitute themselves to their gods and sacrifice to them, they will invite you and you will eat their sacrifices. And when you choose some of their daughters as wives for your sons and those daughters prostitute themselves to their gods, they will lead your sons to do the same.

However, despite Solomon's great gift of wisdom, he failed miserably in being careful to listen and obey God's word in his later days. Let us investigate this aspect of Solomon's life more closely.

There are five RESULTS that come from turning one's heart away from God.

    I. A Lust for Many Wives

    II. A Lust for Many Idols

    III. A Judgment from God

    IV. A Rise in Adversaries

    V. A Rebellion from Within

A Lust for Many Wives – 11:1-3

Solomon had failed to heed two of God's commands: he was not to take multiple wives, and he was not to intermarry with the Canaanite women. Unfortunately, Solomon's failure to heed God's injunction against intermarrying with the unbelieving Canaanites who did not put their faith in the Lord, was not only injurious to Solomon, but it would also affect the children born in the coming generation and perhaps be repeated in others for generations to come. This became immediately apparent in the case of Solomon's son Rehoboam, who succeeded him, for his mother was an Ammonite woman (14:21c, 31). Rehoboam's mother's name was Naamah and guess what? She apparently was also a pagan and an unbeliever!

While it is true that Solomon may originally have taken foreign wives as a way of cementing many of his diplomatic alliances with other countries, it was also clear from the text that Solomon also "held fast [Hebrew, *dabaq*, 'cleaved'] to them in love" (2). Therefore, the diplomatic alliance explanation quickly evaporated as Solomon became emotionally involved in an improper attachment to these same women, who also eventually led him away from the God he had professed such love for in his earlier days. Seven hundred wives and three hundred concubines may be a secular way of showing off the splendor of his kingdom, but it also directly led to his downfall and was an outright disobedience to God's word.

It is more than just a matter of curiosity that the passages admonishing Israel to "love" the Lord and to "cling" to him in Deuteronomy 10:12; 11:22; and 30:20 contain the very same words used of Solomon's "love" for his wives; he "held fast" or "clung" to them and he "love[d]" them as the text clearly describes as his error (1 Kgs. 11:2). Surely Solomon had moved far from the position he had taken earlier in his life, where he "showed his love" for the Lord (3:3), to a position where now he was more concerned to show his love for his wives than his love to Yahweh.

Notice how frequently the term "heart" appears in vv. 2-4: it appeared some five times! However, its use here is different from our western usage that usually stresses only our emotions and feelings; instead in Scripture there is more of an emphasis on the thinking, willing, and loving center of a person in the use of this word. In fact, the Bible seldom, if ever, separates the heart from the head (a person's brains or mind from the will of their internal being), but instead it sees the head as acting in the heart. Thus, when we speak of the "heart," we are not dealing exclusively with what is the invisible and internal part of an individual, even though it all begins inside the heart of each person. Long before we see the external aspects of where a person is going in life, we note that the root of it all was born within. So, the internal is foundational, but it also has external manifestations in real life as well. Moreover, what had first taken place in the heart did not happen overnight, or as a sudden surprise, for Solomon's plunge into compromise took years to take root until it broke out in full bloom and a constant drift away from the Lord.

A Lust for Many Idols – 11:4-10

The standard by which Solomon was measured was the life of his father King David. If ever a man had a paternal model that he could emulate, God called David "a man after [his] own heart." David did fail in the Bathsheba incident, but he also quickly repented under the mentorship of the prophet Nathan, and asked God for his forgiveness.

Now instead of following the Lord, Solomon "followed Ashtoreth, the goddess of the Sidonians, and Molech the detestable god of the Ammonites" (5). So reprehensible was "Ashtoreth" that the writer deliberately distorted her name from its regular spelling of "Astarte" to "Ashtoreth," which involved a re-vocalization of this goddess' name by inserting the vowels "o" and "e" in her name taken from the Hebrew word for "shame," *bosheth.* Indeed, such idolatry was a "shameful" practice, for she was the well-known Canaanite fertility goddess. Her worship involved fertility rites in the high places and in the shrine that Solomon built for her worship.

No less disgusting was "Molech" or "Milcom" idol worship, which used the Hebrew consonants *mlk (i.e., malik,* "king"), and seems to be the same worship that was found observed in the transplanted colony of Phoenicia in North Africa named Carthage. This deity may have been the same as the Canaanite deity named elsewhere as Baal, who required human sacrifice of children to himself (2 Kgs. 16:3; Jer 19:5; 32:35). Connected with Molech was a sacred enclosure named "tophet," a Syrian word that meant "fire pit." Children were dropped alive into the fire pit, no doubt a flame that was set to burning inside the image of Molech. It was a disgrace and an abomination to high heaven and one that cried for justice on the part of the lives of the babies and young children that were snuffed out as they rolled down the arms of Molech while they were still alive, only to drop into the burning fire pit inside the idol! For example, in the city of Carthage, infant sacrifices to Molech abound with thousands of jars of small bones buried in a cemetery there.

Another detestable god worshiped in Moab, named Chemosh, was honored as a god, along with the god Molech. Both were mentioned in this passage (7) because of the extremely abominable practices that each of them stood for and the gods his foreign wives honored. They symbolized how far the king had fallen. But even worse was the statement that was attached to these notices about the two idolatrous deities: "[Solomon] did the same [idolatrous worship] for all his foreign wives, who burned incense and offered sacrifices to their [foreign] gods" (8).

One would think that if the Lord, who had personally appeared in Gibeon to a person on two separate occasions, as he had to Solomon, then they certainly would have lived differently for the rest of their lives, but this was not so for Solomon. Instead, because of the special privileges and blessing he had enjoyed, he was even more culpable for his sin. Solomon could not claim that he lacked evidence of God's love or his favor; he had experienced an enormous outpouring of God's favor and real evidence of his love. In fact, he had been chosen for the position of king, in what many would have judged to have been almost a last-minute close call to his losing the throne to his brother. Furthermore, he had been also named *Jedidia*, by the Lord himself, meaning "loved by the Lord." Considering his gift of wisdom, the abundant blessings offered to him, and all the riches, wealth and reputation God had given to him, it is impossible to say that he had not been distinctively gifted and blessed by God.

Nevertheless, "The LORD [with a more than justified reason] became angry with Solomon because his heart had turned away from the LORD, the God of Israel, who had appeared to him twice" (9). But in this reaction, God was merely following his policy outlined in Deuteronomy 6:14-15. He had warned that he was a jealous God and that his anger would burn against those who departed from him. His jealousy did not mean he was green with envy or anything like that; instead, it meant his desire was so directed towards the good, just, and right, that all evidence of sin stirred his emotions deeply. He had forbidden Solomon to follow other gods, but Solomon paid little attention to God's command (10). What then had happened to the model his father David had set before Solomon to follow earlier in his life? Had David ever sinned in such a manner as this? Where had the exemplary modeling that David had provided gone in the meantime? But we too must be asked: How many times have we provoked our Lord despite his repeated evidence of love and blessing?

A Judgment from God – 11:11-13

Verse 11 taught that Solomon's sin was also in an "attitude," for there was an attitude expressed in Solomon's failure to keep God's covenant and his decrees (11b). As a result, God would "tear" the kingdom out of the hands of his son Rehoboam when he came to the throne at the time of Solomon's death in 931 B.C.E. (11c, 23-33).

This threat, however, was immediately qualified in vv. 12-13 by the stricture that God would place on this judgment: "for the sake of David your father," the entire kingdom would not be lost to him. Even with this loss of some of the territory belonging to the original kingdom of Israel, God would still "not tear the whole kingdom from him, but [he would] give one tribe for the sake of David [his] servant and for the sake of Jerusalem, which [God] had chosen" (13). The "one tribe" given to Solomon's son referred to the tribe of Judah, of course, while ten tribes were "torn" away and given to the Northern Kingdom, which broke away from the tribe of Judah (31, 35). Later, Benjamin would join Judah to complete the 12-tribe pattern, as 1 Kings 12:20 makes clear. But what happened in the meantime, so that Benjamin was left outside of the mentioned eleven tribes? The best answer seems to be that Bethel, Ramah and Jericho became part of the northern ten nations, i.e., those towns that were part of the northern portion of Benjamin, while the southern part of Benjamin joined the tribe of Judah. Also, the tribe of Simeon, whose inheritance had been scattered throughout Judah, eventually migrated north sometime after the division of the kingdom and in 2 Chronicles 15:9 and 34:6, Simeon is listed with the tribes of Ephraim and Manasseh in such a way that they seemed to be part of the northern tribes by now. Thus, Judah and a portion of the original Benjamin merged to form the southern kingdom of Judah.

A Rise in Adversaries – 11:14-25

Solomon had seen adversaries previously, for that is what he had faced when he came to the throne of David, but at that time, God had put them all aside, because his blessing was on Solomon and because Solomon had purposed in his heart to follow the Lord. But no longer was the blessing of God on Solomon, for now the Lord himself was raising up political and military adversaries against him (14). In rapid succession, God raised up the following:

"Then Yahweh raised up against Solomon an adversary, Hadad the Edomite" (14).

"And God raised up against Solomon another adversary, Rezon [king] of Aram" (23).

"Also, Jeroboam son of Nebat rebelled against the king. He was one of Solomon's officials" (26).

The first of three strong men that God raised up as adversaries against Solomon was "Hadad the Edomite." The closer Solomon got to the end of his reign, the more nettlesome these three adversaries became to the peace of his kingdom. Earlier, David's army had defeated the Edomite army by slaughtering 18,000 men (2 Sam. 8:13-14; 1 Chron. 18:12-13) over a period of six months. Why Joab had been so determined to wipe out the Edomite army is not known (1 Kgs. 11:15-16), but Hadad had managed to escape David's victory when he was but a lad (17a). Hadad fled to Egypt, with some of the Edomite officials who had been in the employ of Hadad's father. So, the seeds of this trouble for Solomon went back in time and had their roots in the days of David.

Hadad and his small retinue traveled by way of the desert through Midian and Paran, but eventually reached Egypt, where they were given political sanctuary, probably under Pharaoh Amenemope (993-978 B.C.E.). When Hadad reached an appropriate age for marriage, he was provided with a wife by Pharaoh Siamun, who reigned from 978 to 959 B.C.E. This wife was the sister of Queen Tahpenes. It is plausible that Hadad's wife was Siamun's sister-in-law. An interesting point to consider, if our identifications are accurate, is that the same Pharaoh Siamun, who gave his daughter to Solomon as a wife, also offered his sister-in-law to Hadad,

Solomon's adversary. Hadad's wife bore him a son named Genubath, who was raised within the palace.

When Hadad learned, while he was still in Egypt, that David and Joab had both died, he begged Pharaoh to permit him to return to Edom. The bitterness of the slaughter of his father and his people still was retained in his mind. He wanted to see that revenge would make things even for him.

In the meantime, God raised up another adversary against Solomon, Rezon, the son of Eliada (23), who had also fled for some reason from Hadadezer, the king of Zobah, whom he had served. Rezon gathered around himself a band of rebels or raiders, who made their headquarters in Damascus. Rezon also became Israel's enemy as long as Solomon lived, which only added to the trouble that simultaneously came from Hadad (25).

Solomon, in his only known military expedition in Scripture, had defeated Zobah and Hamath, going as far as the city of Tadmor, also known as Palmyra, an oasis on the caravan route between Damascus and Mari, near the Euphrates River (24c). Rezon probably did not move into the kingship of Damascus until Solomon was in his declining years.

A Rebellion from Within – 11:25-43

A third, but far more dangerous adversary for Solomon came in the person of an Israelite named Jeroboam. Jeroboam came from the tribe of Ephraim, where he was first noticed as part of the Ephraimite labor force that was working on the "supporting terraces" in Jerusalem, also known as the Millo, where there was a breach in the wall of the old city of David. So effectively did he carry out his tasks that he came to the attention of Solomon, who put Jeroboam in charge of the whole contingent from Ephraim and Manasseh, "the house of Joseph" (28). The Scripture labeled him "a man of standing," (Hebrew, *gibor hayil),* meaning he was exceptionally industrious, capable and a mighty man of valor.

It was somewhere in this period, as Jeroboam was going to Jerusalem, where he was still overseeing the Millo construction project, that the prophet Ahijah from Shiloh met him along the way. When the two of them were alone in the open country, the prophet Ahijah took his own new raiment and tore it into twelve pieces (30) and invited Jeroboam to take ten of the pieces (31). Ahijah then explained the prophecy to Jeroboam: God was going to tear the kingdom out of the hands of Solomon and give Jeroboam ten of the twelve tribes (31b). However, because of God's love and respect for David, Yahweh would give one tribe to Solomon and his descendants.

God repeated the reason for this action: it was because David and the city of Jerusalem had forsaken him and worshipped Ashtoreth, the goddess of the Sidonians, Chemosh the god of the Moabites, and Molech the god of the Ammonites, and he had not walked in the ways of the Lord, nor done what was right in God's eyes (33).

However, God presented Jeroboam with an opportunity to establish an enduring dynasty of his own in northern Israel (37-38). But the conditions laid down for him were the same ones that God had laid down for the Davidic dynasty: "If you will do whatever I command you and walk in my ways and do what is right in my eyes, by keeping my statutes and commands as David my servant did, I will be with you. I will build for you a dynasty as enduring as the one I built for David and will give Israel to you. I will humble David's descendants because of this, but not forever" (38-39).

It was clear that the promise God had made to David was continuing, but the ten-tribe nation was being offered to Jeroboam if he would only walk pleasing to the Lord. Judah did experience a series of tragic loses in the days that followed, for in the fifth year of Rehoboam's reign (c 925 B.C.E.), after Solomon had died, Pharaoh Shishak came and took all the wealth David and Solomon had accumulated back to Egypt as booty. Judah became smaller and smaller as she was reduced almost overnight from being the world's greatest kingdom to now a little kingdom with little or no power at all. But things would not remain that way forever, for the Davidic covenant (2 Sam. 7), and the Biblical prophets spoke of a glorious day coming when the twelve tribes would be reunited and the people of Israel and Judah would be restored to their land and Messiah would reign on the throne of David forever.

Solomon did attempt at some earlier point in his career to murder Jeroboam, but Jeroboam quickly fled to Egypt, where he stayed with Pharaoh Shishak until Solomon's death (40). The cause for Solomon's wrath against Jeroboam seems to have been in an attempted rebellion against Solomon (26), but no details are given, and Jeroboam had to flee to await the proper timing before the prophecy of Ahijah could be realized.

Conclusions

1. Not all who begin well finish well in life. What is needed is a daily dependency on the grace of God and the need for a walk with God that showed his "obedience of faith" to carry out what he showed as he began in his reign so well.

2. All other loves that take the place of our primary love for God are totally out of place for the believer and eventually will lead us astray from our Lord.

3. When God warns about idolatry and religious intermarriages that are outside the faith, he not only wants the best for us, but he also wants to spare us from learning by experience what he had warned us about what would happen in that eventuality in the first place.

4. When we depart from the Lord, God loves us so much that he will bring every pressure he can to help us cry out in our lost-ness and pain until we call for his help and we come back home to him again.

Questions for Thought and Reflection

1. Of what nations did the Lord warn Solomon not to take a wife from? What danger did the Lord see in such marriage arrangements?

2. How does "a heart fully devoted to the Lord" evidence itself in the life of a leader or in the lives of his followers?

3. What sinful building project that Solomon engages in on the hill east of Jerusalem? For whom did Solomon design this? Why did he not make the same provisions in the city of Jerusalem for the same persons?

4. Why was the worship of the god Molech particularly offensive to the Lord? What in our current world is so much like this worship?

5. When Solomon engaged in such offensive indulgence in worshiping other gods, why did God still favor him? What was the evidence of that favor? Does this show an inconsistency in the character of God?

6. Of the three adversaries that the Lord raised up against Solomon, which one turned out to be the most offensive with the longest lasting results for the future of the nation Israel?

Lesson 8

Solomon's Psalm of the Extent of Messiah's Rule and Reign

Psalm 72:1-18

"The greatest block of predictive matter concerning the Savior to be found anywhere in the Old Testament," according to J. Barton Payne, "is in the book of Psalms."[1] He found 101 verses in the Psalms of direct Messianic prophecies in thirteen different Psalms. Other writers tended to be more conservative in their estimates, such as the Lutheran commentator H. C. Leupold, who limited the number of Messianic Psalms to four: Psalms 22, 45, 72, 110.[2] At the other extreme was St. Augustine, who unfairly treated every Psalm as if it were messianic. But his approach violated the basic rules of exegesis, for it is better to rely on the straightforward claims of the text itself than to depend on a spiritualized or allegorical sense to the words.

In our treatment of Messiah in the Psalms,[3] we argued for thirteen messianic Psalms: 2, 16, 22, 40, 45, 68, 69, 72, 89, 109, 110, 118, and 132. This is very similar to the list given by James E. Smith,[4] but he argued for sixteen such Psalms. Thus, he added Psalms 8, 78:1-2 [sic], and 102.

As we have often described these Psalms arranged in the order of the predictions made in the life of Messiah, the following suggested order is as follows:

David's Greater Son, Messiah – Psalms 89, 132

The Rejection of Messiah – Psalm 118

The Betrayal of Messiah – Psalms 69, 109

The Death and Resurrection of Messiah – Psalms 16, 22

The Written Plan and Marriage of Messiah – Psalms 40, 45

The Triumph of Messiah – Psalms 2, 68, 72, 110

---

1. J. Barton Payne. *Encyclopedia of Biblical Prophecy.* New York: Harper and Row, 1973, p 257.
2. H. C. Leupold. *Exposition of Psalms.* Grand Rapids: Baker, 1974, pp 21-23.
3. Walter C. Kaiser, Jr. *The Messiah in the Old Testament.* Grand Rapids: Zondervan, 1995, pp. 92-135.
4. James E. Smith. *What the Bible Teaches About the Promised Messiah* Nashville, TN.: Thomas Nelson, 1993, pp 90-209.

Psalm 72 is called a direct Messianic Psalm because it uses the future tense throughout the Psalm and because of the frequent use of the figure of speech called hyperbole. Even King Solomon, who wrote this Psalm, could not have fulfilled its terms in all his glory. Instead, Solomon's reign can supply only the imagery, language, and line of descent through which the one and only Messiah will rule and reign in that future day.

Psalm 72 is one of the "Royal" or "Kingship Psalms," which Hermann Gunkel (1862-1932) described as such in his *Die Psalmen* (1926-28).[5] Gunkel had proposed ten Royal Psalms according to their literary forms: Psalms 2, 20, 21, 28, 45, 72, 101, 109, 132 and 144:1-11, but it did not seem that Psalms 101 or 110 met his own criteria. Much later, John H. Eaton used the criteria that Gunkel argued for identifying two of his Royal Psalms, by showing that they had a Davidic superscription, as he went on to develop some twenty-four additional characteristics for this category of Psalms, resulting in a list of fifty-four Royal Psalms, which he then added to Gunkel's original list of ten Royal Psalms.

Surprisingly, nowhere in the New Testament is Psalm 72 quoted or treated as a Messianic Psalm. Nevertheless, so clear is the picture of the king described in this Psalm and so extensive and far-reaching are the boundaries of his rule and reign, not to mention the similarities seen between this Psalm and Isaiah 11:1-5 or Isaiah 60-62, that one cannot deny that Psalm 72 is Messianic and indeed a Royal Psalm.

Another clue to its Messianic interpretation is the use of metaphoric and hyperbolic language that clearly extended the limits of the royal reign well beyond the boundaries of Israel and the times of Solomon, or any other Davidic king for that matter. It is this use of hyperbolic language that brings us to a dialogue with the Antioch School, which was founded by Lucian of Antioch (d. C.E. 312), and who was followed by such imposing names as Theodoret of Mopsuestia (circa C.E. 350-428), Jerome (ca C.E. 347-420) and John Chrysostom (ca C.E. 347-407) in this line of thought.

The Antiochene School established the model for what they called the "Theoria" view, which meant in the Greek the "sight," "insight,"

---

5. Much of the material that follows is an expansion of my article, "Psalm 72: An Historical and Messianic Current Example of Antiochene Hermeneutical *Theoria*," JETS 52/2 (June 2009): 257-70.

"vision," or the lining up of what had happened in the past with an analogous final event in the distant future, so that they could be said to be one in meaning, even though there might be two or more events in the future fulfillments. The work of Bradley Nassif's Fordham University dissertation,[6] on the method of theoria, has been especially helpful to me in analyzing this Psalm.

The Antiochenes, as is well known, stood over against the Alexandrian School, which latter school used the allegorical method of interpreting the Scriptures. But the Antiochian School grounded all meaning in the historical reality of the past, which often served as a mirror by which one could see the future lined up in the same single meaning, so that the past and the distant future were part of the same single vision.

It was Julian of Eclanum who seems to have best learned the principle of theoria from Theodore, while living with him from C.E. 421-428, after his being exiled from Italy. Theodore demonstrated the method of Theoria in the way the Apostle Paul used Hosea 1:10 ("And it will come about that, in the place where it is said to them, 'You are my people,' It will be said to them, 'You are sons of the living God.'" In Romans 9:26 Julian taught, therefore:

> The apostle wants to show us which rule we must follow in the interpretation of the prophetic books. It is this: That when [we hear the prophets] speaking about the Jews, [and] something is promised that goes behind the small circle of people, yet we see it partly fulfilled in that nation, we know from *theoria* (*per theoriam*) that the promise is given for all people.... It will not be appropriate to say that the recall from the Babylonian captivity is predicted according to history, and the liberty given by Christ [is] according to allegory. No. The prophet predicted both things together at one time, jointly (*cum sermo propheticus solide utrumque promiserit*) in order that the mediocrity of the first fulfillment would predict the abundance of the second ... So, what Hosea was saying about the Babylonian times, Paul [likewise] attributes to the facts of the Savior.[7]

---

6. Bradley Nassif. *Antiochene Theoria in John Chrysostom's Exegesis* (Ph.D. dissertation, Fordham University, New York, 1991).

7. Ibis., 55. Nassif cited it from the Latin in A Vaccari, "La '*theoria*' nella scula esegetica di antiochia," <u>Bib</u>. 1 (1920):20-22. The English translation is one Nassif commissioned.

This approach to interpreting the Old Testament prophets is very similar to the method used by Willis J. Beecher's method of "Generic Interpretation." Beecher did not use the term *theoria*, but he defined his parallel method of interpreting prophecy in this way:

> A generic prediction is one which regards an event as occurring in a series of parts, separated by intervals, and expresses itself in language that may apply indifferently to the nearest part, or to the remotest parts, or to the whole – in other words, a prediction which, in applying to the whole of a complex event also applies to … its parts.[8]

This is not to say that the Antiochene School or Beecher were teaching "double meaning," or "double sense," as if the historic meaning meant one thing in the past and in the future fulfillment it intended another meaning; instead, that is precisely what both were clearly trying to avoid. Therefore, they argued for one sense, one meaning, even though there often were multiple fulfillments of that same single meaning of the text that was shared hyperbolically or analogically.

The Canonical Placement of Psalm 72

Several commentators have investigated why certain Psalms are placed on the "seams" or divisions of the five books of the Psalter. Furthermore, what patterns of organization can be discerned from the placement of the Psalms if there is one to be found at all.

Walter Brueggemann and Patrick Miller[9] noted that the placement of Psalm 73, which appears at the beginning of Book III (Psalms 73 – 89), stands in juxtaposition to Psalm 72, a Psalm authored "By/for Solomon," that ends Book II in the Psalter. If this was done intentionally, which we believe, they were deliberately placed that way. Then why were the two Psalms placed back-to-back? If Psalm 73 is a sapiential, or wisdom Psalm, as most contend, and Psalm 72 is a royal psalm, does the juxtaposition of the two Psalms have more meaning and significance than immediately meets the eye?

---

8. Willis J. Beecher. *The Prophets and the Promise.* Grand Rapids: Baker 1963, 1970, repr. Of 1905 ed., p 130.
9. Walter Brueggemann and Patrick D. Miller, "Psalm 73 as Canonical Marker," *JSOT* 72 (1996):45-56.

G. H. Wilson, however, argued for precisely that point when he claimed that there was a progression in the royal psalms placed at the seams of Books I – II of the Psalter. In these psalms it was possible to chart the rise and fall of the Davidic monarchy. Thus, for Wilson,[10] Psalm 2 marked the inauguration of the Davidic Covenant, while Psalm 72 marked its transition to a future line of Israelite kings, leaving Psalm 89 (at the end of Book III) to lament what had happened to the rejection of that line (even if only temporarily from an evangelical point of view) of the Davidic kings. Some think this also explains why the Royal Psalms plays such a small role in Books IV to V when compared to their larger role in Books I- III.

Christopher Seitz[11] has taken this argument one step further. He proposed to view the Davidic House and kingship of God as portrayed in Psalms and Isaiah as being parallel to one another. Therefore, as the Davidic throne *recedes* into the background and then finally *disappears*, as it appears to do from the Fall of Jerusalem in 586 B.C.E. onwards, the kingship of God *rises* in prominence from there on, instead. Accordingly, Psalm 72 is to be viewed as a fading marker of the Davidic line, thereby allowing the emergence of the Enthronement Psalms about God in Book IV (Pss. 90-106) to take center stage.

It is directly in answer to this pitting the Davidic Dynasty opposite the coming enthronement of Messiah that makes a return to the Antiochian hermeneutic of *theoria* to be so useful. Instead of reinterpreting or contrasting the promised throne of David with the rule of Messiah, one can still insist on retaining the full historical setting and meaning of Psalm 72, centering on the Davidic kingship, while noting that the Psalm's hyperbolic progression of a conscious enlargement of that concept, involving a progression from the seminal idea as given to David and his house, into its final realization in the ultimate Davidic king, the Messiah. The text itself will be the best place to test this thesis.

---

10. G. H. Wilson, "The Use of Royal Psalms at the 'Seams' of the Hebrew Psalter," JSOT 35(1986):85-94.
11. Christopher Seitx, "Royal Promises in the Canonical Books of Isaiah and Psalms," in *Isaiah in Scripture and the Church* (unpublished manuscript, 1994) referred to in Brueggemann and Miller, "Psalm 73," 51, n. 17.

There are three ways we benefit from the rule of Messiah.

I. By Observing How Righteous and Fair the Messiah is to All

II. By Noting How Extensive and Beneficial the Messiah is to the Whole World

III. By Sensing How Prosperous and Blessed Messiah is to All

By Observing How Righteous and Fair the Messiah is to All – 72:1-7

Many have wanted to view Psalm 72 as composed of four poetic strophes based on what they perceive as four themes of the king's and Messiah's reign; it was a reign that was: (1) righteous (72:1-7), (2) universal (Ps 72:8-11), (3) beneficial (72:12-14), and (4) perpetual (72:15-17). For example, James Smith argued for these same four qualities of Messiah's future reign.[12] But a better case was made by Charles A. Briggs for only three strophes, each beginning with a prayer by Solomon in verses 1, 8, and 15.[13] In Brigg's view, the three prayers corresponded to Solomon's prayer for wisdom offered at Gibeon and his prayer at the dedication of the Temple. This seems to be the best division of the Psalm; therefore, the exposition of this passage will follow that structure for our teaching and preaching.

The imagery and content of this Psalm is prompted by the peaceful and prosperous reign of the grandest monarch Judah ever had, King Solomon. It is this historical reality that had served as the basis for anticipating a surpassing hyperbolic expression of such a greater reign in the future, but which had only been seen in modest glimpses experienced by the Davidic King Solomon. It is not as if Solomon cherished the wish that he in his person would finally epitomize, or even perhaps that he would be that coming Messianic person himself; rather, Solomon speaks here as a prophet who anticipated one who would come after him and who would be greater than he ever was or ever could hope to be (cf. Matt. 12:42).

Psalm 72 begins with a prayer to God that is signaled by its vocative form. "O Elohim!" "Elohim" was the divine name that embraced all nations and all of creation, along with all its creatures in its address,

12. James Smith. *What the Bible Teaches...*, p 195.
13. Charles A. Briggs. *Messianic Prophecy.* New York: Charles Scribner's Sons, 1889: pp 137-40.

whereas "Yahweh" usually assumed a personal relationship with the people who were believers. Even though this Psalm may originally have been created for the coronation ceremony of Solomon, as some argue, nonetheless much of the content of the verses that follow extend well beyond that single setting, so that they could hardly be understood of any earthly monarch except by way of pure "hyperbole."[14] This, of course, was one of the reasons why Believers have treated this Psalm as Messianic, as well as being one that historically refers to Solomon.

With this prayer, Solomon continued with a demand ("give," i.e., "endow," in the imperative mood) that Elohim would endow the king with the concept and gift of justice. The verbs used here are best understood as future tenses, rather than the jussive forms for "may, or "let." These verbs request that God would indeed grant such a request to "a king" (Hebrew, *lemelek*), not "the king." The scope of this request is enlarged by making "a king" parallel to "a son of the king" (Hebrew, *leben melek*). The concern of the psalmist is the whole royal house of David as climaxed in Messiah himself be gifted in the same way.

The only use made of the divine name in this whole psalm is Elohim. Elohim was requested to endow the king with two divinely originated virtues: "God's justices" (note the rare plural) and God's righteousness. The plural of the word "justice" probably signified justice in the fullest form of God's decisions and judgments, while the gift of his "righteousness" pointed to what was right, harmonious and normal in all relations between God and mortals as determined by the character and attributes of God. This righteousness is mentioned three times in just three verses (1-3). It included the concept of God's law and the state of being in conformity with all that is good, excellent, and that which maintains what is "in-the-right" with the will and work of God. The hope expressed here is that this endowed king will continue to dispense these gifts for a long time to come.

It is at this point where the author's hyperboles begin to manifest themselves as extending over a duration of such a time of peace, prosperity and divine vindication that they would extend "as long as the

---

14. So commented Mitchell Dahood. *Psalms vol. 2:51-100.* AB; Garden City, NY.: Doubleday, 1968, p 179.

sun and as long as the moon last" (v. 5). It is important to recall, however, that this very same concept of perpetuity is what had been promised specifically earlier in the Davidic Covenant (2 Sam. 7:13, 16).[15] The psalmist's prayer request, then, is that God would make happen all he had promised to David in the Davidic Covenant.

In addition to these requests, the peace and prosperity of the kingly reign is likened to "rain falling on a mown field" (v. 6). This too is not an unexpected metaphor in a Davidic or Messianic context, for it has already been used of the refreshing effects of the reign of a Davidic king in 2 Samuel 23:3b-4 ("When one rules over men in righteousness, when he rules in the fear of God, he is like ... the brightness after rain that brings the grass from the earth.") It is also worthy of special note that the fertility of any country or land is connected to the righteous rule and reign of a just and fair king. It is important to note how frequently the concepts of "rain," "growth," and "fertility" are linked with the concepts of "right," "righteousness," and "justice" in the Scriptures. These sets of attributes cannot be separated if peace, justice and righteousness are to prevail in any country.

By Noting How Extensive and Beneficial Messiah is to the Whole World – 72:8-14

The extent of the just king's kingdom stretches from "sea to sea" and "from the River [Euphrates] to the ends of the earth" (v. 8). This would cover everything from the Mediterranean Sea on the west of Israel to the uttermost sea on the earth and from the Euphrates River (for so the Hebrew spelling here demands by its usage the Euphrates River) unto the ends of the earth – an obvious set of hyperboles! In part, there is also an allusion to the boundaries of the promise land (Exod. 23:31, where it was announced that, "I will establish your borders from the Red Sea [Yam Suph] to the Sea of the Philistines [Mediterranean Sea] and from the desert to the River [Euphrates]"). However, the kingdom of Messiah will far

---

15. For further elaboration on this point, see Walter C. Kaiser, Jr., "The Blessing of David: The Charter for Humanity," in *The Law and the Prophets: Old Testament Studies in Honor of O.T. Allis*. Ed. John H. Skilton. Phillipsburg, NJ.: Presbyterian and Reformed, 1974, pp 298-318.

exceed anything ever seen in the Judean line of kings. Messiah's kingdom would reach the fringes of the civilized world, embracing the desert tribes, and it would even subjugate all "enemies," who would suffer defeat as they "lick[ed or bit] the dust" (v. 9), as had been predicted against Satan himself in the earliest announcement of the Promise-Plan of God, later called the Protoevangelium in Genesis 3:14-15, and repeated for all the Davidic kings' enemies in Isaiah 49:23 and Micah 7:17a ("Nations .... Will lick dust like a snake, like creatures that crawl on the ground").

But there is more: the reign of this righteous king would extend as we have seen thus far: (1) *geographically* from sea to sea, which is to say around the world; (2) *militarily* over all enemies opposing his reign; but now add to this that this reign would extend (3) *economically*, as tribute and gifts will be brought from all over the world (v. 10); and (4) *politically*, so far as all potentates will come under this righteous king's rule and serve him (v. 11). Nations far and near will come bringing gifts to him, much as the Magi did when Messiah appeared in his first advent. Another example of the nations coming from abroad can be seen in the reference to "Tarshish" (v. 10), long identified with Tartessos in southern Spain, but more recently as Tarshish in Sardinia. "Sheba" and "Seba" (v. 10) are located respectively in modern Yemen is South Arabia and in an African nation (cf. Gen. 10:7; Isa. 43:3; 45:14).

The blessed king will invest himself on behalf of the needy, the afflicted, the weak, and the oppressed along with those who are victims of violence; in other words, he will take up the cause of those who are destitute and cast aside by society at large (vv. 12-14). Their lives ("blood" in v. 14) are precious in that coming king's sight. While King Solomon may have carried out some of this while he was king, it is clear, at least by the end of his reign, the ten northern tribes felt that Solomon had treated them badly, for they felt overtaxed and handled unfavorably in comparison with the tribe of Judah. It would be no surprise then, that Solomon's son, King Rehoboam, was unsuccessful in addressing the grievances against the later years of Solomon's reign. Moreover, Solomon's reign never took in all the world's needy, poor, and oppressed; someone greater than Solomon was needed to finish the job.

By Sensing How Prosperous and Blessed Messiah is to All – 72:15-17

For a third time, the psalmist's prayer is enjoined for: (1) the unending perpetuation of the Davidic dynasty; (2) the security and economic thriving of the kingship; and (3) the extension of the king's great wealth in all areas of life. Once the conditions mentioned in verses 12-14 had been met, then the longevity of the just and righteous king could be described. This can be illustrated in the gifts that come from the subject nations, such as "gold from Sheba" (v. 15; cf. 1 Kgs. 10:14-15). Sheba, of course, is the land from which the queen came to visit and test Solomon's wisdom (1 Kgs. 10:1-13). It is located at the southwestern tip of the Arabian Peninsula in modern Yemen.

Even though God had given fruitfulness to the land of Israel during Solomon's day, still the prayer for the days of the coming of Messiah were ones in which they would be accompanied with an abundance of grain throughout the land in such proliferation that the stalks of grain would wave just as plentifully and beautifully as the trees of Lebanon, even from the most unexpected, but usually desolate places; namely, with the poorest growing conditions on the tops of the mountains (v. 16). As A.A. Anderson put it:

> This verse (v. 16) and the Psalm as a whole, shows that what we call the "moral realm" and the "realm of nature" form one indivisible whole to the Israelites. A community which lives according to righteousness enjoys not only the internal harmony but also prosperity in field and flock.[16]

Some read, instead of "his name" in verse 17, "his progeny." But this is not well supported by the text. The truth of an extensive "seed" is taught abundantly in other contexts (Isa. 9:2; 49:20; Zech. 2:8[4], but in this context it is the name of the Lord that is lifted high.

The use of the Hebrew Hithpael of the verb *barak*, "to bless" (v. 17b), is usually rendered reflexively, i.e., "bless themselves," as if all the nations of the world will see what is happening to Israel as they too will bless themselves! But this Hebrew form can be read just as well as a passive form of the verb, "will be blessed," as can be seen in two of the five instances where it appears in the same promise made in the Abrahamic Covenant (to Abraham: Gen. 12:2-3; 18:18; 22:17-18; to Isaac: Gen. 26:3-4; and to Jacob: Gen. 28:13-14), which all use the Hebrew passive form of

---

16. A. A. Anderson. *The Book of Psalms*. 2 vols. New Century Bible Commentary. Grand Rapids: Eerdmans, 1972, p 525.

the verb in the same expression. To this day, most commentators remain skeptical about the passive meaning of the Hebrew Niphal (used in three of the five cases in the patriarchs), much less the Hebrew Hithpael (used in two of the five cases). However, O. T. Allis's 1927 article presented strong evidence to the contrary, which article has not been answered to this very day.[17]

Book II of the Psalms in which this Psalm itself ends with a doxology in verses 18-20, attributes to the Lord all the blessings that already have or will come from the reign of God's anointed one. The Lord is the worker of "marvelous deeds" or "wonders," a word that was also used of God's works in the plagues of Egypt against Pharaoh.

There is little wonder then that Isaac Watts (1674-1748) and James Montgomery (1771-1854) composed two hymns based on Psalm 72.

Watts wrote:

> Jesus shall reign where'er the sun
> Does his successive journeys run:
> His kingdom spread from shore to shore,
> Till moons shall wax and wane no more.
> People and realms of ev'ry tongue
> Dwell on his love with sweetest song;
> And infant voices shall proclaim
> Their early blessings on his name.

Montgomery wrote:

> Hail to the Lord's Anointed.
> Great David's greater Son!
> Hail in the time appointed,
> His reign on earth begun!
> He comes to break oppression,
> To set the captive free,
> To take away transgression,
> And rule in equity.

---

17. O. T. Allis, "The Blessing of Abraham," *Princeton Theological Review* 25 (1927): 263-98. See also Walter C. Kaiser, Jr. *The Promise-Plan of God: A Biblical Theology of the Old and New Testaments*. Grand Rapids: Zondervan, 2008, especially pp 17-67.

Conclusions

1. The words of the psalmist are the same in both history and prophecy, for what they saw in a vision (theoria) held both the historical point of view in unity with the hyperbolic expressions that took them beyond the historical situation to the ultimate fulfillment.

2. David's line would finally produce a king who would rule with justice and righteousness as he defended the afflicted ones, the poor, and the needy in the last days.

3. Under Messiah's rule and reign, peace, prosperity and righteousness would be the order in that day.

4. All the kings of the earth would come to bow down before Messiah and to offer him their gifts as his rule endured forever as long as the sun and moon endured.

Questions for Thought and Reflection

1. Judged on your reading of Psalm 72, do you think Solomon understood that his line of descendants was in the Messianic line, ones who would rule as long as the sun and the moon endured?

2. How extensive do you think Solomon pictured his kingdom reaching when he wrote this Psalm under the inspiration of God?

3. How wide and broad do you think Solomon's understanding of the mission of the good news was to the Gentiles?

4. What is included in the divine promise-plan of God's covenant with Abraham, Isaac, Jacob, and David found in Psalm 72?

Lesson 9

Enjoying the Blessings of Messiah's Rule and Reign [1]

Psalm 127

King Solomon is credited with composing only two Psalms found in the Psalter as we have already noted. However, it is surprising that the New Testament nowhere quotes Psalm 72 as a Messianic Psalm. Yet despite this fact, there is a clear picture of the coming King Jesus described in this Psalm. For example, so extensive are the boundaries of Messiah's reign, and so similar is some of the wording between this psalm and prophecies in Isaiah such as Isaiah 11:1-5 and Isaiah 60-62 that the grounds for assigning this psalm as a Messianic psalm can hardly be denied. Even granting room for the hyperbolic and metaphorical language in this psalm, the limits of Messiah's reign go well beyond the boundaries of Israel as we saw in the last chapter. Thus, Psalm 72 simultaneously celebrates the reign of an illustrious and exalted king in the day when this psalm was written, as well as it reflects the advent of coming ruler who will distinguish himself in a reign of peace, righteousness and benevolent concern for the poor, oppressed, and disadvantaged in a future day as well.

There are two endeavors which are futile without God's assistance.

I. The Futility of Household Management Without God

II. The Futility of Marriage and Raising Children Without God

The Futility of Household Management Without God – 127:1-2

Everything in life, not just the building of houses and palaces, depends on God's blessing and protection. It is from this psalm that many houses have inscribed near their entrances the Latin clause: *Nisi Dominus frustra,*

---

1. Much of the material in this chapter first appeared in my article "Psalm 72: An Historical and Messianic Current Example of Antiochene Hermeneutical Theoria," *JETS* 52/2 (June 2009): 257-70.

"Except the Lord builds, we labor in vain." The Germans call this *haushallten*, "managing the household," but Aristotle (Politics 1.3-13) entitled it *oeconomia*, which is the same as our word "economics." But Solomon, who wrote this psalm, according the ancient title in this heading of Psalm 127, wrote here similar words to what he had said in Ecclesiastes 9:11, i.e., if God withholds blessing, it doesn't matter how swift, wise, strong, brilliant or learned one is, the battle will be lost, because the battle belongs to the LORD!

Therefore, when Solomon refers to "building the house," he is not referring simply to the material construction of a home, but he refers instead to everything in connection with life in the home. The economy of a household includes all relationships in a household, such as that of the master to those employed around the home, a husband to a wife, a father to his children, as well as other relationships, such as those engaged in the gaining property or getting wealth. Solomon's purpose was not to take us into house construction methods, but his purpose was to describe a believer's marriage and how all in that household should conduct themselves as fellow heirs of the grace of life.

The American dream is that anyone who works hard enough can realize anything they really put their hearts into doing, but Solomon puts a strong caveat to that line of thinking. He urged, instead, that all in that household should put the Lord first and seek his blessing, otherwise it will all be for nought. Three times the words "in vain" appear in vv. 1-2. The futility of mere human activity is set forth in five useless pursuits: the labor of building a house, the act of guarding a city, the act of rising early to go to work, the other act of staying up late to finish your work, and the constant eating food earned by hard labor. If God is not in these activities, they constitute a vain exercise and it will all be "in vain," or just so much repetitious boredom that suggest only that change is the only constant in a life lived apart from God.

Solomon was the consummate statesman and master builder, but he also realized that without God all was a big waste of time and energy. For thirteen years Solomon built his own house and related buildings, but for seven more years he also built God's house. Likewise, he also fortified cities and built city gates over which archaeologists still marvel over their design and strength. But he strongly asserted his utter dependence on the Lord in just as strong terms. No matter how diligent he was, or we may be, except the Lord prosper the work of the worker's hands, we will end up failing to make any significant despite all our industriousness and diligence. We must depend on God's graciousness and covet his blessings for our marriages, our families and the success of our labors.

Martin Luther became the first teacher to successfully revolt against the tyranny of the Church Fathers and the Scholastic writers of the Middle Ages, who allegorized this psalm rather than adhering to its straightforward literal teaching, for he restored Psalm 127 to its full dignity and beauty. Thus, began one of the greatest social revolutions that Europe had known up to that time, for now marriage and the family were restored to the place God had appointed them to be in. Luther wrote:

> This passage alone should be enough to attract people to marriage, comfort all who are now married, and sap the strength of covetousness. Young people are scared away from marriage when they see how strangely it turns out. They say, "It takes a lot to make a home;" or "You learn a lot by living with a woman." This is because they fail to see who does this, and why he does it; and since human ingenuity and strength know no other recourse and can provide no help, they hesitate to marry. As a result, they fall into unchastity if they do not marry, and into covetousness and worry if they do. But here is the needed consultation: Let the Lord build the house and keep it, do not encroach upon his work; the concern for these matters is his, not yours. .... Does it take a lot to make a house? So what? God is greater than any house. He who fills heaven and earth will surely also be able to supply a house, especially since he takes the responsibility upon himself and causes it to be to his praise. (Luther, *Works*, 45:324).

Even Augustine and Chrysostom depicted domestic life as being secular and common, a veritable hindrance to all spiritual life. In their poor views, if one were to strive for spiritual perfection, one had to abstain from marriage and devote oneself to celibacy and retire from the world. But then the very joys to which this psalm speaks of would be denied and overlooked. This psalm and its twin, Psalm 128, must *not* be treated as a set of allegories of divine relations and joys, as if the "wife" was allegorically equal to the "believers," the "spouse" equal to Messiah and the "shoots" were allegorized to speak of the sons and daughters of God!

To be sure, this text does not say, "The Lord builds the house, so there is no need for anyone to work!" There is work involved, but not needless worry and covetousness that is being commended here. The kind of work, however, that is being criticized is the kind that implies or boasts, "I did it all by myself." That is what "is vain" and "futile," – in short, what is plain boring and redundant in its repetitiousness. See how Solomon commends work in the book of Proverbs 6:10-11; 10:4, 22; 12:24; 20:4: 24:30-34. Usually, God gives us very little unless we work for it, but in his allowing us to work for it, we should not forget his goodness to us, nevertheless. Luther asked: Who put the silver and the gold in the mountains? Who fertilized the soil of the field that is ripe with grains and grapes and all other sorts of produce? So, it remains, "Unless the Lord builds the house, its builders labor in vain." When other economic theories delete this principle, they find out to their sorrow how different things can be apart from God.

What was said of the house is now said of the city and the nation. Let the people found a city and establish a nation and ask if that city or nation forget to live under the guidance of the Living God, it must be asked: Will that city or nations endure for very long? It is futile to think that nations or cities can make it on their own; they can't (Ps 33:10; 94:11; Dan 4:35).

The Futility of Marriage and Raising Children Without God – 127:3-5

It seems as if suddenly the psalmist has lost his train of thought, or that he has incorrectly attached another psalm to vv. 1-2. But if that is not so, then what is the connection between vv. 1-2 and 3-5?

The comparison seems to be between the arrogant, anxious, and distrustful person who gets up early and works late, but it is all for nothing. But the humble, calm and trustful person who is at rest with his lord and his world can sleep whether things are good or bad. Consequently, a "heritage" and a "reward" await this person (3-5).

It turns out that more than my livelihood, my housing, my job, my breath, and my nation's security are gifts from the Lord; even my children are not the result of my own powers. The conception of a child is wholly the work of God. Thus, whether we possess anything or not is gift of God.

Solomon compares children with "arrows in the hands of a warrior" (3). Thus, just as a warrior shoots his arrows wherever and whenever he chooses, so God deals with us! It is amazing to see what extraordinary stature in life comes to some who have never striven, for it is God who is working behind the scenes and thus things turn out more differently than we had thought.

While our children are still at home as dependent ones, God still guides these "shoots" and "arrows" as he wills. He is vitally concerned about them from the cradle through all those years of adolescence and into maturity (4). Even the blessedness of a full "quiver" (5) is honored in this text. The recognition that children are gifts is not a mundane or secular approach to spiritual things; it is the Bible's full embracement of all things as coming from the hand of God. Thus, these principles are to be applied to our lives:

1. Don't be stingy about the number of children we wish to have if God so directs, for we may only be cheating ourselves, and the Lord who wishes to give us an inheritance.

2. Don't put off having children until our assets are more stable and we have money to give them all the finer things in life. Children were meant to increase our effectiveness, not diminish it. Remember, unless the Lord builds the family, we labor in vain.

3. Children are the best retirement plan around. No one will put us to shame in the city gate when so many children will come to our defense, for they are our inheritance and reward if we need them to speak up for us

Happiness for each household, then, rests in trusting the Lord, for unless he builds the house, the family, the city, the nation, we will all work and strive to no avail.

We conclude this psalm and study with another of Isaac Watts' arrangements, this one of Psalm 127:

If God succeed, not all the cost
And pains to build the house are lost;
If God the city does not keep,
The watchful guards as well may sleep.

What if you rise before the sun,
And work and toil when day is done,
Careful and sparing eat your bread
To shun that poverty your dread;

'Tis all in vain, till God hath blest;
He can make rich, yet give us rest:
Children and friends are blessings too,
If God our sovereign make them so.

Happy the man to whom He sends
Obedient children, faithful friends:
How sweet our daily comforts prove
When they are seasoned with His love!

Conclusions

1. To build or to attempt anything without the advantage of the presence of the Lord on our side is an exercise in futility.

2. Guards watch over a city to defend it, but that city will come to calamity unless the city also trusts in the Lord for its defense.

3. It is likewise pointless to get up early or to stay up late to finish the tasks that are piling up against us if we seek no assistance from God.

4. Numerous children are given to married couples as a gift from the Lord.

5. It is good to have the blessing of many children, for when the parents are old, they will not face shame or the opposition of enemies alone or without the support of our children.

Questions for Thought and Reflection

1. Based on what this Psalm claims, why is that some who exert themselves almost to a frazzle seem to get nowhere?

2. In what ways can a town or city claim that the Lord is watching over them to guard them? How certain can cities be of this claim? Does that mean that those towns or cities need not prepare to arm themselves for a defense of their possessions?

3. According to this Psalm, why is that so many in America suffer from insomnia? What remedy exists to the believe for insomnia?

4. Children are regarded increasingly as just pains in the neck in today's culture. Does this Psalm agree and why does it take the position it takes?

5. What kinds of blessings are inherited by those with large families? Should we Believers advocate for large families or not?

6. How does this Psalm show that God had granted to Solomon wisdom?

Lesson 10

Solomon's Heavy Tax Load and His Son's Decision

1 Kings 12:1-33

Solomon had certainly accomplished much during his reign, but it may have come about through a heavy taxation program on the people. Thus, we are given the background in I Kings 12:1-3a for the way the government continued for Solomon's son Rehoboam after his father's death, and the rebellious innovations of King Jeroboam's setting up of two golden calves in Bethel and far north in Dan (12:25-33) as northern Israel's new gods. In between these two anchor points two sections of Rehoboam's consultation with the elders and the younger generation (12: 4-15; and 16-24).

There are four awful choices Rehoboam and Jeroboam made that nevertheless did not frustrate the plan and purpose of God.

I. A Stupid Decision Despite the Sovereignty of God – 12:1-11

II. An Incorrect Decision in Light of the Promise of God – 12:12-20

III. A Decision to Fight That Opposed by the Word of God – 12:21-24

IV. The Arrogance of a False Religion – 12:25-34

A Stupid Decision Despite the Sovereignty of God – 12:1-11

Now that Solomon was dead, it was time for Israel to choose another leader to guide them into the future. Solomon's son Rehoboam decided it would be politically wise to go north to the city of Shechem for his installation where all Israel could make him king (1). He must have felt that already there was some strong criticism of his father's government, so in a move perhaps to pacify the northern ten tribes, Rehoboam went to Shechem, a site that also had roots that went back to the early days of the patriarch Abraham. However, another player in the events that were to unfold came on the scene, for he was the man his father Solomon had attempted to kill, causing him to flee into Egypt (11:40); this new player was the one whom the northern delegation then sent to Egypt to summon him to come back home just as the government was going through a transitional time in the governance of Israel.

Jeroboam and the whole assembly of northern Israel had made a major plea with Rehoboam to give them tax relief from the way Rehoboam's father had laid the tax burden on them in the former days (12:4). They promised if Rehoboam would ease up on the heavy yoke that had been laid on them, then they would serve Rehoboam as his servants. Rehoboam was likely surprised by this request, as Solomon had already been heavily involved the nation in his numerous projects. So, he asked for a three-day reprieve as he took time to think their request over and to gain as much counsel as possible. Patiently, the people went away from Shechem for three days and then returned after that time to hear the king's decision.

Meanwhile, the king had consulted with the elders of Israel who had served his father Solomon as to how they would answer this plea from the people. They thought there was a lot of good sense to what the people were asking for. In fact, they urged Rehoboam to serve the people, for if he did, the people in turn would serve him and be his servants (12:7). Their advice was that a little restraint given "today" (7a) will win the allegiance of the people "all the days" (7b). In other words, use a little honey, not the whip of the workman's overseers, will win more friends and servants to help the nation!

But this advice did not please Rehoboam, so he consulted the young men he had grown up with (8). There is no hint in the text that these younger men had any official status in Israel. The younger bucks, apparently feeling their oats, argued that harsh threatening from the king would subdue the people's implied intimidation of the crown, so they gave a course memorable one-liner Rehoboam could use on the masses: "My little finger is thicker than my father's waist" (10c). Even though many translators have guessed that what they meant by "my little" was his "finger" (which is not stated in the text), but since the rest of the one liner is to the middle of one's body ("waist/loins"), they probably were using a course rejoinder – to which they all must have laughed heartily and boisterously. It was all one big joke, since the younger bucks felt it now was their time to get a chance to govern. Rehoboam, accordingly, coached by the young guys he grew up with in his generation, decided to warn that even though his father had indeed imposed exceedingly heavy burdens of the people in the past, he would increase that by scourging them not just with whips, but with scorpions.

An Incorrect Decision in Light of the Promise of God – 12:12-20

After the three days had ended, the people returned to learn what the king decided (12). As already hinted at in this passage, the king by-passed the advice of his father's elderly counselors and instead used the harsh language of the younger men to really show the people who was king around there (13-14). But why did things go this way? Are these not the people of God? Was not the Sovereign Lord ruler over all?

But v. 15 is quick to tell us that the events of those days were not in the hands of mere mortals. Rather, "the king did not listen to the people, for that turn of events was from the LORD, to fulfill the word that Lord had spoken to Jeroboam the son of Nebat – words that had come through the prophet Ahijah the Shilonite" (15; 1 Kgs. 11:29-30; 2 Chron. 10:15). True, the decision and responsibility for all that had happened was clearly to be charged to the guilt of the human participants, yet none of what was happening was catching God by surprise and messing up his purpose and plan for the ages! (1 Kgs. 11:33).

The peoples' response, however, was immediate, for it was clear to them that the king had rejected their requests and was not going to give them any relief. So, the cheer of dismissal went up from those from the ten northern tribes:

"What share have we in David,
what part is Jesse's son?
To your tents, O Israel!
Look after your own house, O David!"

Even though God had already decreed long ago what was now taking place. King Rehoboam was still fatally responsible for what he had done. The northern ten tribes must have been prepared for the worse to happen, but that is exactly what took place. There was no hope that Rehoboam would relieve any of the harsh burdens he had imposed on them. So, those Israelites who came from the northern ten tribes broke off from Judah's control of them, while only those still living in the south remained under Rehoboam's rule (17).

To show that Rehoboam did not possess any of his father's wisdom or good sense, he decided to send Adoniram, the officer in charge of forced labor in Israel under the United Kingdom, to impose the will of the Judahite king (18). But the people of the ten northern tribes stoned him to death and Rehoboam was fortunate to get to his chariot and escape back to Jerusalem alive. Thus began the rupture between the north and the south in Israel that lasts to this very day. But Rehoboam, stubborn as he was, still did not get it, for he returned to Jerusalem and called an assembly of the people from Judah to make him king. He was going to be king one way or another, and this was another! But it was clear that only Judah remained loyal to him (20).

But Rehoboam had one more stupid trick up his sleeve. He mustered the whole house of Judah, and at least part of the tribe of Benjamin, to go to war with the northern house of Israel and thus regain the kingdom for Rehoboam (21). Rehoboam got together 180,000 fighting men, but fortunate for him and the people of the nation of Israel, God send a man of God named Shemaiah to the king and this is what that prophet said to Rehoboam: "This is what the LORD says: 'Do not go up to fight against your brothers, the Israelites. Go home, every one of you, for this is my doing.'" So, in Rehoboam's first wise move in this whole series of events, he decided to listen to what God had said through the prophet Shemaiah and not go to attack the north. Rehoboam was saved from one more act of folly.

Dale Ralph Davis in his commentary on this passage tells the humorous story of how William Jennings Bryan was defeated in his third bid to win the USA Presidency in as many tries. Bryan illustrates his failures by relating another story about the fellow who under the influence of strong drink tried three times to gain entrance into a private club, but was repeatedly thrown out of the club and down the stairs leading to the club each time he tried to get in. After he landed in the street after his third unsuccessful attempt to storm the club, he picked himself up, dusted off his clothes and said with as much poise as was left in the situation: "They don't fool me. Those guys [just] don't want me in there."[1]

Jeroboam's Arrogance of a False Religion – 12:25-33

Jeroboam, the newly returned renegade from Egypt, had no doubt learned much from his years of serving in Solomon's administration before he fled to Egypt. So, he probably knew he had to act quickly and wisely to build an administrative structure before the people would also get dissatisfied with him and give back their allegiance to Rehoboam (26-27). He relieved the people of the hated corvee service that David and Solomon had set up. But he immediately went to rebuilding and equipping Shechem as his capital city as well as the city of Peniel, thereby giving him protection against any Aramean invasion from the north or northeast (25).

Jeroboam knew that if the people of his kingdom continued to go to Jerusalem to offer sacrifices at the Temple, eventually Rehoboam would once again win their allegiance and they would no doubt kill him, Jeroboam, and return to serve King Rehoboam. So, Jeroboam sought the advice of his people, who must have advised that he set up two golden calves to provide their own national place of worship, one at Bethel and the other at Dan, which use of golden calves must have been a flash back to what had happened at Mount Sinai (Exod. 32:4, 8). Now, even though the Lord had spoken in favor of the political split of the kingdoms, there was no direction given from heaven that the nation should be split religiously and theologically. Thus, an alternative and more local substitute for the peoples' religious expression would be better served

---

[1] Dale Ralph Davis, *The Wisdom and the Folly: An Exposition of the Book of First Kings,* Ross-Shire, Great Britain, 2002, p. 134.

politically and by the convenience of proximity if they had their own place of worship. A center was, therefore, conveniently set up at Bethel and another was provided for those in the far north at the town of Dan (28-29). Excavations at the archaeological site of Dan have preserved for our day the existence of a high place for the altar and worship of one of the golden calves.[2]

Jeroboam fabricated a whole new religious order that paralleled the Levitical order given by Moses. He appointed priests from all sorts of people, even though they were not Levities (31). Most of the real Levites, however, left the north and went into the sphere of Judah's service. Jeroboam also instituted an annual feast for the fifteen days of the eighth month, rivaling Judah's Feast of Tabernacles that fell on the seventh month in Jerusalem (32). It was clear that Jeroboam was not trying to follow the laws and festivals of Scripture, but he was determined to defy and break all the commandments of God. His reign, therefore, was just as much under the judgment of God as that of Rehoboam. Had Solomon failed in raising his son Rehoboam?

---

2. See the photographs from A. Biran, *Encyclopedia of Excavations in the Holy Land,* Oxford: Oxford University Press, 1977m 1:320.

Conclusions

1. Rehoboam failed to follow the example of his father Solomon. Instead, he exhibited his own folly at almost every major decision-making point until God sent a prophet who stopped him finally at that juncture.

2. Rehoboam went to be installed as king in the northern city of Shechem, perhaps thinking he could win over the northern ten tribes who by that time had had enough of his heavy corvee and taxing methods.

3. Rehoboam followed the advice of the young bucks rather than the advice of the elders who had served with his father Solomon.

4. The north chose a man whom Solomon had chased away from his government to lead their ten northern tribes, whose name was Jeroboam.

5. When Rehoboam was about to open a war with the northern ten tribes, a prophet named Shemaiah warned that this rupture in the tribes was from the Lord.

Questions for Thought and Reflection

1. Why did Jeroboam and his people select the golden calves as the best objects for their worship? What impact do the sins of the fathers have on their children?

2. Reflect on Rehoboam's decision to go to Shechem to be installed as king. Is there a historical reason for such a choice? Is ceremonial ritual as important as looking after the needs of the people?

3. Why was Rehoboam so dense in his thinking that he could not see that the people really were suffering under their required labor [power and taxes?

4. Why did the northern tribes refer to the Judahites as the "house of David" and not to Judah? Was this a denial of the doctrine of Messiah as well?

Lesson 11

The Man of God and
the Old Prophet

I Kings 13:1-34

Our chapter begins by suddenly telling us that a Man of God came north from Judah to the city of Bethel where he found King Jeroboam standing by an altar, that no doubt had one of the two golden bulls associated with it. Suddenly the man of God, sent north by the word of the LORD, burst on the scene with a cry: "O altar, altar! This is what the LORD says: 'A son named Josiah will be born to the house of David. On you [O altar], he will sacrifice the priests of the high places who now make offerings here, and human bones will be burned on you.'"

What a way to begin a ministry! Along with the message just delivered, the Man of God from down south in Judah, gave a sign: "This is the sign the LORD has declared: the altar will be split apart and the ashes on it will be poured out" (13:3). It was bad enough that the altar had been cracked in two, but added to that was what appeared a most unusual follow up to that division of the altar; there was a violation of the Levitical law which required that the ashes from the altar were to be removed and carried off to a clean place for their disposal (Lev. 1:16; 4:12; 6:10-11). But the way this happened, and all at the command of the word of the Man of God, left no doubt that this was nothing less than a desecration of the altar. Therefore, when the ashes spilled out of the altar on to the ground, it thereby rendered both the altar and the services upon that altar both unclean and not pleasing to God. Was this God's indication of his disapproval of what Jeroboam had concocted as a rival institution for the worship of the LORD? Did the Man of God from the south dramatically do this as a public demonstration that Jeroboam and his newly invented types of priests with altars near golden bulls was not approved by God. Let us look at the passage in more detail.

There are three signs that God's word is not to be trifled with or disobeyed.

I. Divine Signs of Disapproval to a Renegade Kingdom

II. Divine Disapproval of Abandoning the Word of the Lord by His Messenger from the South

III. The Lying Old Prophet and Jeroboam Both Abused the Word of God

Divine Signs of Disapproval to a Renegade Kingdom – 13:1-10

The Man of God came north with the distinctive message from God that the altar of this false place of worship would be "torn" (Hebrew, *qara'*) in two, just as God had told Solomon that he would "tear" his United Kingdom from him (1 Kgs. 11:11, 12, 13; cf. 11:30). Perhaps this ripping the altar in two would bring back to Jeroboam's mind the prophecy the prophet Ahijah had given to him in 1 Kings 11:30. If so, then perhaps Jeroboam got the point that the altar at Bethel signified a "torn" religion as well; one that was under judgment!

This sign, however, was not the only sign this prophet gave to the newly installed king Jeroboam, for the Man of God gave at least four other signs to Jeroboam that day to make sure he got the message. These signs were the following ones:

He gave to King Jeroboam first a sign of his "power," for when the king stretched forth his boney finger and commanded, "Seize him," his hand immediately shriveled up, so he was unable to draw back his arm. That must have been enough of a shot over the king's bow to impede him from trying to harm his prophet. God sent a clear message that Jeroboam should not challenge this Man of God, or he would face severe consequences beyond his shriveled arm.

A second sign we can call, along with Dale Ralph Davis,[1] a sign of "truth" (13:3, 5). This sign was one that bore not only present truth, but it spoke of a future, which turned out to be some 300 years later in time when it would happen. Its meaning was that a son of David named "Josiah" would come along and he would take the human bones of

---

1. Dale Ralph Davis, *The Wisdom and the Folly,* p. 152.

Jeroboam's deceased fake priests and burn those bones on that ruptured altar. That is exactly what happened, for 2 Kings 23: 12, 15-18 records this fulfillment to the prophecy given by the Man of God:

> "**12** He pulled down the altars the kings of Judah had erected …., **15** even the altar at Bethel, the high place made by Jeroboam son of Nebat, who had caused Israel to sin – even that altar and high place he demolished. He burned the high place and ground it to powder and burned the Asherah pole also. **16** Then Josiah looked around, and when he saw the tombs that were on the hillside, he had the bones removed from them and burned on the altar to defile it, in accordance with the word of the LORD proclaimed by the Man of God who foretold these things. **17** The king asked, 'What is that tombstone I see?' The people of the city said, "it marks the tomb of the Man of God who came from Judah and pronounced against the altar of Bethel the very things you have done to it." **18** 'Leave it alone,' he said, "Don't let anyone disturb his bones."

There can be little doubt that the prophecy made by this servant of God was long remembered and in detail, for when King Josiah inquired about a certain tombstone, the people knew exactly to whom it belonged and what the owner of that tombstone had said almost three centuries prior for that. They told Josiah it belonged to that Man of God who had spoken against the altar at Bethel exactly what king Josiah had just done to it! Josiah responded with, "Leave it alone."

The Lord gave to King Jeroboam a third sign, which was a sign of "grace." Accordingly, when the Man of God interceded for his shriveled-up hand, the LORD restored that hand (13:6). No way did Jeroboam deserve such a gracious move from the Lord, given his conduct at that altar in Bethel, but nevertheless God was still gracious to him. You would think that that would have enough of a motivation for King Jeroboam to change his thinking, acting, and ways, but no such response is seen in those days. Jeroboam was quick to plea for the prophet to pray for him, but when God answered that prayer, he felt no obligation to turn to him in repentance.

The fourth and final sign was a sign of "repudiation" (13:7-9), for when he offered to show at least some appreciation for the prophet's prayer for the healing and restoration of his shriveled up hand, he invited the prophet to "Come home with me for a meal, and I will give you a gift" (7). But the prophet saw there was no change of heart, so he bluntly refused the royal invitation, for he knew that Jeroboam was trying to buy him off.

The Man of God was on to Jeroboam's ways, for he answered him, "Even if you were to give me half of your possessions, I would not go with you, nor would I eat bread or drink water here. For I was commanded by the word of the LORD: 'You must not eat bread or drink water or return by the way you came'" (13:8-9). Obviously, this divine command was a sign that the northern kingdom was under a divine judgment, therefore the prophet was not to touch their food or water. But we are never told why he was instructed to take another route from the road he had come to Bethel on. Could it be that the Lord knew he was going to test his prophet by sending that old prophet after him? The Man of God, in fact, did take another route home, but he stopped to sit under an oak tree (13:14). Why did he do that when Bethel was a mere six miles to the Judean territory? We have no indication why he stopped short of his goal. This exposed him to an attack from the evil one and made him a "sitting duck" for what was now to happen to him.

Divine Disapproval of Abandoning the Word of Lord by His Messenger from the South – 13:11-24

Now there lived at Bethel an old prophet with his sons. Why they were living there if he was a real prophet of God cannot be answered. The old prophet was not present the day Bethel had a strange visit from the Man of God from Judah, but his sons were there and heard everything. Why the boys attended such a false cult event is also beyond explanation, but they gave a report to their father the old prophet who asked, "Which way did he go?" (12). The sons knew which way, for they had seen him leave. So, the old prophet had his sons saddle up his donkey and off the old man went in pursuit of him. He caught up with the Man of God sitting under an oak tree. The old prophet asked if he was the Man of God who had come from Judah (14), to which he replied he was.

Now here is where the story gets a bit tricky, for he urged the Man of God to return to Bethel with him. The Man of God repeated his rejection of the offer in the same terms he had given to King Jeroboam. But the old prophet informed the Man of God that he too was a fellow clergy member who had received a word of the LORD from an angel to invite to return with him to Bethel. However, we are told flat out: "But he was lying to him." (18b). So, the Man of God returned with the old Prophet. But why would this lie to the Man of God? What could be an appropriate motive for such an act? How then, just minutes later, he had the chutzpah to announce that the Man of God had defied the word of the LORD? (21). Moreover, the old prophet correctly predicted that the Man of God's body would not be buried in the tomb of his fathers (22), for the Man of God had not kept the command God had given to him (21b).

The Lying Old Prophet and Jeroboam Both Abused the Word of God – 13:25-34

This passage raises a ton of questions for us, for there are many details we are clueless about. But one thing is clear: the passage refers to the "word of Yahweh/LORD" nine times (13:1, 2, 5, 9, 17, 18, 20, 26, 32). To these texts we may add other references to the LORD's speaking (13:3, 21) and it becomes increasingly clear that the "word of the LORD" is the theme of this passage. That can be accepted as the rock-bottom truth in this text.

What happened to the Man of God on his renewed start for home in Judah really puzzles us even more. For as the Man of God went on his way, "a lion met him on the road and killed him, and his body was thrown down on the road, with both the lion and donkey standing beside it" (24). But this was not a normal lion attack, for if it had been such, there would have been evidence that the lion had feasted on the Man of God's body and perhaps a traumatized donkey as part of the scene. But it is necessary for the end of this story for the lion and the donkey to remain standing perhaps motionless over the dead man's body and the nearby donkey, lest the whole episode be simply passed off as just another example of how dangerous the roads had become as of late. Our Lord, however, wanted to call attention to this whole series of events as one of the great turning points in the history and life of a nation. That would explain the solid planting of the lion and donkey beside the victim, for this was no usual happening, but one that involved the strong arm of the Son of God.

Moreover, the Bible does teach us in other places that someone may be the instrument through which God accomplishes his will and yet be blameworthy for his carrying out that even. Davis points to Mark 14:21 where the act of the disciple Judas is an example of this principle: "For the Son of Man goes as it is written of him, but woe to that man by whom the Son of Man is betrayed!"

Perhaps this principle helps us, for in an amazing way, the old prophet did speak the truth of God (20-22), but he also was instrumental in destroying the life of one of God's servants. Can both good and bad come from the same source?

The Old Prophet picked up the dead body of the Man of God and took him back to Bethel where he buried him in his own tomb (29-30). Then the old Prophet, presumably with his sons, mourned over him, saying "Oh my brother." (30). Nevertheless, we must say in conclusion: "What a strange story!"

After they had buried the Man of God's corpse, the old Prophet demanded of his sons, "When I die, bury me in the grave where the Man of God is buried; lay my bones beside his bones. For the message he declared by the word of the LORD against the altar in Bethel and against all the shrines on the high places in the towns of Samaria will certainly come true" (31-32). But if this was true, as it was indeed, then why had the old Prophet spun the lie that entrapped the Man of God? Was he also judged by God for the role he played? The text never commented on that point.

Sadly, despite this manifestation of the power and grace of God, King Jeroboam did not change his ways. He merely continued to appoint anyone who wanted to be a priest could be one. Thus, the downfall of the nation of the ten tribes was set from its very beginning. It would be destroyed from the face of the earth. (33-34).

Conclusions

1. We should never doubt in the darkness what God has said to us in the light. The word of God remained true and without addition or subtraction regardless of where those additions or subtractions came from.

2. God had tried to warn the northern ten tribes from the very beginning that they were on a track bound for judgment if they did not turn around and repent.

3. The Man of God gave enormously important predictions of what the people would face in years to come. King Josiah came some 300 years later and carried out all this anonymous Man of God had predicted.

4. The Man of God obeyed all he had been told up to the letter when he was accosted by the old prophet who claimed to have a more recent word from God that countered what he had been previously told.

Questions for Thought and Reflection

1. Why do you think the Man of God took time on his way back to Judah to sit under an oak tree when he was so close to home?

2. Why did the Lord specifically tell the Man of God to take another route home from the way he had come – much as the wise men were to take another route home, thus avoiding a return to Herod's palace? Was he riding on a donkey and was his, or had he borrowed it from the old prophet?

3. What possessed the old prophet to dream up the lie he invented? What was he trying to do, as far as you can tell?

Printed in the United States
by Baker & Taylor Publisher Services